Endorsements

"Mitch Luse shares about marriage and life as he lives it, genuinely and powerfully. His perspective sets the insightful tone of value and purpose that husbands need. He beautifully reveals, like an architect, God's intended plan for this foundational relationship. Mitch exposes the subtle indulgences that trap us in cycles of smallness and deception and applies rugged honesty to free us from ourselves. And he does us a favor: he goes first. We see ourselves in him and as we find courage, we also find the heart of what this thing called marriage is all about. This book is refreshing. It's absolutely true. And it summons a response from its readers."

—John Leach
Executive Pastor,
Life Center Ministries International

"This book, *The 5:25 Call: God's Design for Husbands*, written by my friend Mitch Luse, is a book that presents a lifestyle that has been discovered and lived out in a very practical way by the author. His journey is not a fairy tale, but a story of a man who is madly in love with Jesus and his wife. You will find amazing insights and practical steps to apply to your life as a husband."

—Dr. Mike Hutchings
Director of Education, Global Awakening

"Interweaving personal experience with biblical and psychological insight, Mitch opens up profound truths and wisdom, especially for his readers who are husbands, although the contents of this book are challenging and inspiring to us all. *The 5:25 Call: God's Design for Husbands* includes reflection questions at the end of each chapter, as well as a declaration and a helpful prayer guide. This has the potential to be a life-changing book in the hearts and lives of men and the women they love. I believe this to be a gift from our Bridegroom God to our great need today."

—Janet Munn
Director, International Social Justice Commission,
The Salvation Army

"Being a husband is a great calling for any man. There are many examples of exceptional husbands all around us, however, the steps on how to achieve success in this area remain vague. Mitch Luse offers transparency and a commitment to truth on God's role for husbands in marriage. Mitch clearly defines the heart, attributes, and thought processes of a godly and exceptional husband. It is very clear that Mitch's heart is to give us clear examples of health in marriage. As his personal friend, it has been a pleasure to watch him live this out in his daily life."

—Kevin J. Pitts
Pastor, His Church Ministries

"*The 5:25 Call* reads like a blueprint of God's design for husbands. A fresh look on the role of the husband and on the call to an intentional, Spirit-filled, healed and set free marriage is precisely what we need today. Mitch Luse unpacks a powerful punch of theological and biblical truths on marriage and then, with vulnerability and sincerity, takes it to the root, intertwining his own story and personal revelation. I can personally attest that Mitch and his beautiful bride Katie have done the hard work behind the scenes, and I have experienced in my own marriage the fruit of walking alongside them."

—Tabitha Swires, Lieutenant
Commanding Officer Bay Ridge Brooklyn Salvation Army,
The Salvation Army

"The Christian life is filled with so many amazing opportunities, experiences, and beautiful promises of God. In an age that celebrates individuality, ambition, and self-promotion, the foundational call to sacrificial love and service is often overlooked. The earth is in desperate need for the sacred office of "husband" to be displayed in all of its glory. Mitch not only beautifully articulates the intricacies of this high call, but also models this in his own life in a way that has deeply impacted me personally. I strongly recommend this fantastic resource for any man looking to model Christ in their marriage."

—Justin Allen
Associate Evangelist, Global Awakening

"This book offers men a fresh and insightful challenge to apply truths derived from stories found in Scripture in our own lives and especially in our marriages. Mitch has drawn from the life of Mary's Joseph principles and actions to help us all pursue greater intimacy and connection with our wives. Because of his willingness to share transparently from his own walk, even the harder challenges feel accessible to us. And adding the prayer guide at the conclusion gives us a means to work this call into our own lives. Taken seriously, I firmly believe this will help to renew relationships which may feel fractured and bring a fresh depth of connection to couples wanting more."

—PHILL OLSON
AUTHOR,
THE OTHER HALF OF THE ARMY – WOMEN IN KINGDOM MINISTRY

The 5:25 Call

God's Design for Husbands

By Mitch Luse

THE 5:25 CALL

Copyright © 2020 by Mitch Luse. All rights reserved.

Unless otherwise noted, all Scripture quotations are taken from the Holy Bible, New International Version®, NIV®. Copyright © 1973, 1978, 1984, 2011 by Biblica, Inc.® Used by permission of Zondervan. All rights reserved worldwide. www.zondervan.com. The "NIV" and "New International Version" are trademarks registered in the United States Patent and Trademark Office by Biblica, Inc.®

Scripture quotations marked ESV are from the Holy Bible, English Standard Version. Copyright © 2001 by Crossway Bibles, a division of Good News Publishers. Used by permission.

Scripture quotations marked GW are taken from GOD'S WORD®, © 1995 God's Word to the Nations. Used by permission of Baker Publishing Group.

Scripture quotations marked KJV are from the King James Version of the Bible.

Scripture quotations marked MSG are from *The Message: The Bible in Contemporary English*, copyright © 1993, 1994, 1995, 1996, 2000, 2001, 2002. Used by permission of NavPress Publishing Group.

Scripture quotations marked NASB are from the New American Standard Bible, copyright © 1960, 1962, 1963, 1968, 1971, 1972, 1973, 1975, 1977, 1995 by The Lockman Foundation. Used by permission. www.Lockman.org

Scripture quotations marked NLT are from the Holy Bible, New Living Translation, copyright © 1996, 2004, 2007. Used by permission of Tyndale House Publishers, Inc., Wheaton, IL 60189. All rights reserved.

Scripture quotations marked NRSV are from the New Revised Standard Version of the Bible. Copyright © 1989 by the Division of Christian Education of the National Council of the Churches of Christ in the USA. Used by permission.

Scripture quotations marked TPT are from The Passion Translation®. Copyright © 2017, 2018 by Passion & Fire Ministries, Inc. Used by permission. All rights reserved. ThePassionTranslation.com.

Visit the author's website at www.mitchluse.com/.

ISBN: 978-1-7355142-0-8

To Jesus:
Thank You for raising me up with You.

To Katie:
What a journey we have been on!
Thank you for your love, friendship, and commitment.
The best is yet to be.

Table of Contents

Introduction 11

1. In the Beginning 15

2. Adam: The Pride of a Husband 27

3. Joseph: The Humility of a Husband 53

4. Jesus: The Love of a Husband 75

5. The Call 99

Epilogue 125

Prayer Guide 127

End Notes 141

Introduction

> Marriage is the beautiful design of the Almighty,
> a great and sacred mystery—meant to be a vivid
> example of Christ and his church.
>
> —Ephesians 5:32, TPT

The words on the pages of *The 5:25 Call* carry the themes that God has written on my heart about being a godly husband. With the gentle yet decisive strokes of His pen, the Holy Spirit has overwritten the story of my life's wanderings with His kindness, and along the way, I believe He has shared with me part of His heart for marriage and given me something to say to husbands.

While these chapters are authentic to my heart, they also carry timeless treasures found in Jesus and throughout the Bible. These treasures are centered around the profound mystery of marriage mentioned in the fifth chapter of Ephesians:

> "For this reason a man will leave his father and mother and be united to his wife, and the two will become

> one flesh." This is a profound mystery—but I am talking about Christ and the church.
>
> —Ephesians 5:31–32

For husbands, specifically, this mystery is inseparably linked to Jesus' example mentioned in Ephesians 5:25:

> Husbands, love your wives, just as Christ loved the church and gave himself up for her.

Mysteries in the kingdom are like gifts from God that He wants us to unwrap. They are seeds of revelation and truth buried in symbolism, metaphor, and story. Jesus often spoke in parables and mysteries, using His creation to teach us about Himself and His kingdom. He told us stories about mixing yeast into batches of dough, planting the smallest mustard seed that became the largest plant, and a bright-eyed person who sold everything to obtain a pearl of great price. Each of these mysteries carry truths that were "hidden since the creation of the world" (Matt. 13:35). It is our honor, privilege, and responsibility to unwrap the gift of God's truth for ourselves. As Proverbs says, it is the glory of kings to search out what God has hidden (25:2).

Many of us are content to leave as a mystery God's view of marriage and the role of husband. We thank Him for the gift, but we fail to unwrap or understand what it is that He has given us. Like a toddler playing with the wrapping paper rather than the gift itself, we fail to go beyond a surface understanding of God's goodness and intimate involvement in our lives. Many of us have missed our Father's heart, and we live in ignorance of the divine and holy gift that marriage really is.

The goal of this book is to unwrap God's view of marriage and God's design for husbands. This priceless gem is found in the text of Ephesians 5, but its themes are woven throughout God's story in the Bible. While there's been much study, discussion, and even debate on the topic of the relationship of man and woman, I believe one very important thing has been largely missing from the conversation: the heart of Jesus the Bridegroom for His bride, the church. To understand men and women, husbands and wives, and the mystery of marriage, the heart of Jesus, our Creator and Designer, must be central.

As a husband and a follower of Jesus, I am inviting men and husbands to lay aside the wrapping paper of cultural norms and take hold of the gift of marriage and our roles as husbands in it. Let's dive into Jesus and His story to discover who He is and who He has created us to be. Through the following chapters, the reflection questions provided at the end of each chapter, and the prayer guide at the end of this book, I invite you to join me in discovering the 5:25 call, God's design for marriage and our role as husbands.

Holy Spirit, I pray that You would touch each reader with transformational power to the glory of Jesus.

Thank you for joining me through the pages of this book.
—MITCH LUSE

CHAPTER 1

In the Beginning

> In the beginning God created
> the heavens and the earth.
> —Genesis 1:1

Our earthen vessels come to attention at the sound of those three words: "In the beginning…." They call our clay-borne beings back to the earliest moments of humanity. In the beginning God began creating and revealing a great work, one which He prepared before the foundations of the world. Like the first colors exploding on a new canvas, He began creating the heavens and the earth.

Out of His heart His mouth speaks, and into the darkness His voice resounds: "Light, be!" (See Genesis 1:3). The volume of our world's existence cracked open as the great Author began telling our story. But just as with any work of art, the Artist's own story is revealed through His creation. When God began writing humankind's story,

He also left an indelible mark of His own story and His own heart—for the stories are connected.

Centuries later, this same Creator who spoke the world into existence entered the canvas of His creation. All things were made through Him yet He became flesh and made His dwelling among us (John 1:3,17). This Word is the expression of God's heart to humankind. He is the light that shines in the darkness, and all of creation points to Him. He is the living Word of God, and His name is Jesus.

Through Jesus, God created and created and created. Without even sleeping, He spoke all manner of things into existence. He created a universe of matter and music, of color and light. He spoke into being a creation that had never existed before—except within His heart. First, He set the scene with broad brushstrokes: He created day and night, water and sky, land and sea. And on the third day, He reflected and shared His own thoughts about His creation: it was good. The stage was set, and the foundational elements were in place.

His work continued with life and energy continually bursting forth. The aliveness of His creation kept exceeding itself. During the day, under the sky, beside the sea, and on the land He continued. "Let the land produce vegetation: seed-bearing plants and trees on the land that bear fruit with seed in it, according to their various kinds" (Gen. 1:11). And it was so. And it was good.

Against the sky He mounted planets and stars to distinguish between day and night, markers of times and seasons. It was so. And it was good. What He speaks happens. What He does is good.

Vitality flooded the sea, air, and land as God invented living creatures: first the birds for the sky and the fish for the sea. Then on the land, God created living creatures of all kinds: "the livestock, the creatures that move along the ground, and the wild animals" (Gen. 1:24).

Each of the living things had their own kind, a family they belonged to. Each had a match or a counterpart. And it was good.

Then the sun rose on the sixth day. It was a special and unique day, set apart even among the first days of creation. On this day, the heart of the Author would be displayed in a unique way as He introduced the story's main characters. Jesus was about to unveil a new type of creature into His creation, and with it He would be revealing part of His own story as well—because this new creation was made to be with Him, to be of His own kind, to be in His family.

THE FIRST HUMAN

> Then the LORD God formed a man from the dust of the ground.
>
> —GENESIS 2:7

The Hebrew word used when God created man is *yatsar*, and it means to make, form, or fashion something. It's the same word used to describe how a potter forms clay.[1] Like a master potter, Jesus crafted the image of Himself within this progenitor of the human race.

In an astonishing act, He set the human apart from the other creatures by breathing His own breath of life into the human's nostrils, "and the man became a living being" (Gen. 2:7). Earth and Spirit collided in the hands of the Creator to form this new creature, a new kind that had never been seen before. And He brought the human from his humble, earthy beginnings into a garden called Eden. It was a place full of delight, vibrant life, and the wonderful presence of the Creator.

As He had done before, God appraised His creation on the sixth day, but on this day something was different. Something was unfinished—the human was alone. And when God observed the man's aloneness, He stated outright, "It is not good for the man to be alone" (Gen. 2:18). Those words still reverberate through creation today, reminding us that in God's appraisal it is not good that there was only one solitary human. It is not good for man to be without his counterpart.

When God gave this surprising appraisal, I can imagine the bewilderment of the angels standing by, perplexed and confused as to what could possibly be not good in God's creation. But the Creator was not troubled by *His* assessment, "for he already had in mind what he was going to do" (John 6:6): "I will make a helper suitable for him" (Gen. 2:18).

And with this sudden plot twist, the Author strategically placed a hitch in His story line, an unprecedented change that further emphasized the importance of what was about to happen. The presenting problem of man's aloneness would be the frame through which God would share a greater depth of His heart and reveal His own precious pearl of great price.

AN UNEXPECTED SOLUTION

In a profound foreshadowing of the One to come, "the LORD God caused the man to fall into a deep sleep; and while he was sleeping, he took one of the man's ribs and then closed up the place with flesh" (Gen. 2:21). As if under anesthesia, the man laid lifeless on the dust he came from while the Author conducted the operation. The Author removed a part of the man's side from his body and then closed it again with flesh. God's solution to man's aloneness required the man to give up part of himself. It was as if He was causing the man's physical body to reflect his emotional aloneness, trueing up his body to his heart. Not only did the man feel incomplete without a counterpart, but his own body was also experiencing the pangs of lack and loss.

From this part of the man, from his side, God formed the woman (Gen. 2:22). And while she was similar to the man in kind, she was also unique from him. The woman had the same Spirit as the man, but she was made from richer raw materials than the earthy soil he came from. The pinnacle of creation was when God formed and fashioned the man and the woman. And yet, in the way that He brought man and woman into the world, He intentionally spotlighted the woman as being special, unique, and prized.

In the Creator's narrative, God had the man lay down his own life, then God opened up the man's side so that his counterpart could emerge. Not only did she emerge, but out of this surrender, the two of them rose together into a new life. This new life was not defined by the man's isolation or aloneness; it was a life of marital bliss marked by their partnership, connection, and union. These prophetic acts rippled out of God's heart, for the story of Adam and Eve pointed to the day when the Creator Himself would step into the story and lay down His own life to be united with His bride.

MARRIAGE

When God fashioned a counterpart for the man, He took humankind from "not good" to "very good" (Gen 2:18; 1:31). The Lord made her "from the rib he had taken out of the man, and he brought her to the man" (2:22). When He brought the woman to him, the man exclaimed, "Finally! Bone of my bone, flesh of my flesh! Name her Woman for she was made from Man" (v. 23, MSG). I can imagine the overwhelming joy, deep gratitude, and relief that Adam felt at the first sight of his wife. He had found his counterpart, his missing piece! No longer alone, the man and the woman found wholeness in their union.

The Author continued, "Therefore a man leaves his father and mother and embraces his wife. They become one flesh. The two of them, the Man and his Wife, were naked, but they felt no shame" (Gen. 2:24–25, MSG). The two of them, who were different but of like kind, were made for union. From one came the two, man and woman. And from these two came a new and glorious one. Vulnerable, intimate, and accepted, they were unashamed. Through their union they became a new creation: two as one, a married couple—a mystery and a glory.

The Author instituted a sacred union between the man and the woman, representing a deep and profound aspect of His own heart. He made sure to record the moment, for it would serve as a testament in the ages to come. Even millennia in the future, Jesus would reiterate the importance of this union: "At the beginning of creation God 'made them male and female.' 'For this reason a man will leave his father and mother and be united to his wife, and the two will become one flesh.' So they are no longer two, but one flesh. Therefore what God has joined together, let no one separate" (Mark 10:6–9). Wrapped up in Adam and Eve's union was something very important to the Author's heart, because His story is about marriage too.

THE ORIGINAL CONTEXT

When God created Adam and Eve, there was a context in which it happened, a geographical and spiritual scene in which their lives were placed. That scene was called the Garden of Eden, and it was a place of both freedom and love. Genesis 2 describes the garden at the time when God had created the first human but had not yet created the woman.

> Now the LORD God had planted a garden in the east, in Eden; and there he put the man he had formed. The LORD God made all kinds of trees grow out of the ground—trees that were pleasing to the eye and good for food. In the middle of the garden were the tree of life and the tree of the knowledge of good and evil.
>
> A river watering the garden flowed from Eden; from there it was separated into four headwaters. The name of the first is the Pishon; it winds through the entire land of Havilah, where there is gold.... The name of the second river is the Gihon; it winds through the entire land of Cush. The name of the third river is the Tigris; it runs along the east side of Ashur. And the fourth river is the Euphrates.
>
> The LORD God took the man and put him in the Garden of Eden to work it and take care of it.
>
> —GENESIS 2:8–15

After creating Adam from dust, God brought him into the garden and blessed him with work. In Genesis 2, God taught Adam about the culture of paradise and about what was expected of him within it. One way God did this was by giving Adam a command, a specific directive from His mouth to Adam's ears.

> And the Lord God commanded the man, "You are free to eat from any tree in the garden; but you must not eat from the tree of the knowledge of good and evil, for when you eat from it you will certainly die."
>
> —Genesis 2:16–17

Out of all the things God could have said, His first recorded words to Adam were about giving him freedom, liberty, and empowerment: "You are free to eat from any tree in the garden." Those words became a reference point for God's relationship with humanity, and with them, He gave us the gift of freedom. God is not interested in controlling people, He did not create us to be robots or slaves. God chose to empower Adam by setting a culture of freedom in paradise.

One way that God illustrated His value for freedom was by giving Adam choices. Not only could Adam choose what kind of food he would eat, but he was also given choices with weightier consequences. When God commanded Adam not to eat from the tree of the knowledge of good and evil, God told him clearly that Adam would die if he did. By doing so, God gave Adam two clear choices. On the one hand, Adam could choose connection and obedience to God that would yield abundant life. On the other hand, he could choose disobedience to God that would result in death. The freedom God gave humanity was so real that Adam would reap the consequences of his choices, for better or for worse. This freedom is a foundation for God's love relationship with humanity, for there can only be love where there is freedom to choose.

The connection between freedom, choice, and love is communicated well by looking at the aspects of a wedding ceremony. Before the wedding, a man and a woman have the freedom to pursue anyone they want. They have more options and choices than they could ever exercise. But at their wedding ceremony, they publicly proclaim their choice to say yes to one person and an unequivocal no to all others. This is the foundational decision on which the rest of their relationship will be built. From a place of freedom and unlimited choices, they choose to severely limit their options and step into an exclusive covenant relationship with one person, their spouse.

Their vows affirm this mutual commitment to exclusivity and sacrificial love. The man and woman willingly sacrifice their options to take hold of this intimate love relationship. Without this sacrificial choice, they would never experience the depth of love God designed for marriage between a man and a woman. The freedom to choose is a hallmark of the most excellent way of love, and when a man and woman use their freedom to step into an exclusive marriage covenant, they cross into the realm of God's purpose for marriage as revealed in the garden.

In the early moments of creation, God spoke directly to Adam. God was not only teaching him about his love relationship with his Creator, but these lessons would also prepare him for the new season of life Adam was approaching. For in the coming chapters of his life, Adam would be given the opportunity not only to choose to love his God but to apply that culture of freedom and love to a relationship he had not yet considered. God was teaching Adam how to love his wife.

THE MANDATE

> Then God said, "Let us make mankind in our image, in our likeness, so that they may rule [or have domin-

ion]…" So God created mankind in his own image,
in the image of God he created them; male and female
he created them.

—Genesis 1:26–27

From the start, God gave man and woman dominion, which means to rule, reign, or dominate.² God made Adam and Eve His beloved image bearers so that "*they* may rule" (Gen. 1:26, emphasis added). They were *co-missioned* by God to rule together, both man and woman. In the same way that Eve was taken from Adam's side and he was incomplete without her, so was their God-given assignment incomplete without both of them having dominion and authority.

As we look at the lives of Adam and Eve, it is important to note that we live in a different culture than they did. Some things that are familiar to us in the twenty-first century, such as sin and the pain of broken relationships, were not a part of their life in the garden. They lived in the pure light and life of communion with God, and it was very good. For us to understand God's heart and intent for husbands and wives, it is important for us to remove our lenses that have been soiled and scratched by our fallen world. By immersing ourselves in the garden before the fall, we can better understand God's intent for Adam and Eve and their relationship.

For example, in the garden, Adam did not rule over Eve; he was commissioned with her. In that garden, God did not say that Adam had dominion over Eve and that she was to do whatever he said; the authority He gave them was to rule the earth, not each other. Eve was not placed invisibly behind Adam and expected to be his subject; she came from his side and belonged there. The commission was given to a man and a woman of authority, a king and a queen. This was a reflection of God's original design and intent for man and woman.

God blessed them together and said to them, "Be fruitful and increase in number; fill the earth and subdue it. Rule…" (Gen. 1:28). Not only were they both to be powerful in their relationship, but they were also commanded to fill the earth with a race of powerful people who would exercise that same dominion.

From the time of their creation, Adam and Eve were a prototype for all of humanity. And from their original commissioning in the garden, the royal son and daughter of God were called to co-reign and co-rule together, side by side.

Through the creation account, God set the stage for His story and brought two main characters onto the scene. In future chapters, He would further reveal the wonders of marital union and the heavenly reality that it points to. While much of His story and heart were yet to be discovered, at the end of the sixth day, He left us with a telling and profound truth: after the creation and commissioning of Adam and Eve, "God saw all that he had made," and for the first time, He said of creation that "it was very good" (Gen. 1:31).

With these words from the Author, the story took another turn, a turn for the better. This celebration of creation came after He fashioned the woman and established the union of man and woman. Since the Author paused His story to recognize this change, we too should pause and take note of what He called very good. It was very good that man was not alone. It was very good that Adam and Eve had shared authority and dominion. It was very good that they were in communion with their God.

Remember this world that the Author called very good, for it contained deep truths about His heart and intent for humanity. Breathe it in and commit it to memory, because His story was about to take a dark, downward turn, and the Garden of Eden would become a distant memory as man and woman reaped the consequences of their decisions in the paradise of God.

CHAPTER 2

Adam:
The Pride of a Husband

> There is a way which seems right to a man, but its
> end is the way of death.
> —Proverbs 14:12, NASB

Sometimes we're so deep in our own messes that we don't realize the hurt and pain left in our wakes. Flailing in the darkness of our own brokenness, the people we hurt most are the ones closest to us.

In our dating relationship before marriage, Katie and I had a strong love for each other. With that love came a deep value for the gifts, passions, and callings we saw in each other. I so valued Katie's gifts for public speaking, prayer, and ministry. I was impacted by her friendship with God, which was like nothing I had ever seen before. But as much as I was impressed by her gifts, faith, and success, I was even more conscious of her heart, of Katie as a person. We had a very strong friendship, and when we spent time together, we felt the wind of God at our back, supporting us, cheering us on, and leading us forward in our relationship.

When we were married, Katie and I launched into a new level of discovery in our relationship. As we explored our newfound identity as a married couple and began to walk out our wedding vows, the rubber met the road for me. This required me to pull the plug on my old solo lifestyle so I could fully embrace the new. On a personal level, my emotional proximity to Katie was scary because she saw the real me. I was uncomfortable with her seeing my fears and quirks, but even more than that, I was insecure, and I began comparing myself to her. Subconsciously, I compared my weaknesses to her strengths. The same amazing gifts, callings, and heart that I celebrated in our dating relationship now felt threatening and intimidating.

DON'T PASS ME

It wasn't a conscious decision, but as Katie and I settled into our first year of marriage, I began to act differently. Instead of cheering when Katie succeeded, I crumbled and withdrew emotionally. Instead of championing her sense of calling, I felt inferior and rejected. I was stuck in a cycle that I didn't know how to escape, one that was erratic and hurtful to Katie. Whenever I felt threatened, I hid myself in silence, avoidance, and emotional absence until finally my pain exceeded my fear of conflict and rejection. Then I exploded in anger, rage, and other manipulative tools. I didn't know how to manage my internal pain, and when I got squeezed by my circumstances, I made a mess of our relationship.

Katie didn't know what to do. The more she succeeded, the more depressed I would get. I told her not to hold back for my sake, but it was getting more and more obvious that I was triggered by her successes. She couldn't win. When she was succeeding on stage, I'd be down, distant, and unable to connect. If the favor didn't include me, it was safer for her to avoid it altogether.

In time, Katie began saying no to opportunities and shying away from things she was called to because of the toll it took on our relationship. When she shined, I spiraled. In her words, it just wasn't worth it for her. I was overwhelmed with feelings of not being enough, fear of being betrayed, insecurity, and low self-esteem. I often became emotionally overloaded and just shut down.

At one point during the early years of our marriage, I came to a sobering realization. I began to see the power that I held and how I was wielding it. I realized that the decisions I was making in my relationship with Katie would not only impact the trajectory of my life but of hers as well. It wasn't okay with me if Katie didn't pursue her God-given call because of me. I didn't want to try to explain to God why I kept Katie back from His call.

My words and actions communicated to Katie, "I support you with my whole heart. Run as far and hard as you want, and I will love and support you no matter what—as long as you don't pass me. If you pass me, then I will punish you through emotional withdrawal, manipulation, anger, and other hurtful behavior." When I began to understand this dynamic, I was embarrassed and sobered, but I was also thankful to be confronted with how destructive my behavior really was.

A few years ago, I witnessed something that captures this dynamic well, and I want to share it with you. This story is part of how God confronted me with my own fallenness as a husband, and I hope that it's as illuminating for you as it was for me. I call it the older sibling complex.

Years ago, when Katie and I lived in Northern Virginia, we went on a walk through our neighborhood. It's something we often did to clear our heads and connect with each other. While on our walk, we noticed a group of kids walking on the sidewalk ahead of us. I observed the two brothers who were leading the way. At first glance, they were walking together side by side. In time, each of them began walking a little faster. Then they began aggressively power walking to be in front. Finally, they glanced over at each other slyly, trying not to be obvious, and then they suddenly launched into a full-on sprint. The older one was leading, but they both ran as hard as they could, each trying to get ahead of the other. As the younger brother began closing in on his older sibling, something happened that's all too unsurprising: with confidence and force, the older brother thrust his arm out like a crossing guard's neon baton, abruptly stopping the younger brother from passing him and effectively putting him in his place.

The older brother just pulled rank, and there was nothing that the younger one could do about it. I imagine that years of living together proved that the older brother could shut down the younger one at will because he was physically stronger and could enforce his judgments. On a whim, the older brother could flex his muscles and stop the younger in his tracks. There doesn't have to be a good reason for doing this. If asked why, I imagine the older brother would say, "Because the grass is green." The older sibling held the power in the relationship, and every so often he flexed his muscles just to make sure no one forgot that he was in charge.

The funny thing is that when I was watching them, the older brother didn't come against his younger brother as long as he wasn't a threat. The only time I saw the older brother play his card of domination was when he began losing the race, or on a deeper level, when he began to feel insecure or afraid.

I imagine that the younger brother could do just about anything he wanted and not draw the wrath of his older brother. But as soon as he crossed that invisible line and touched one of the older brother's insecurities, he would know it by the unpredictable and unmerited punishment unleashed on him.

Over time, I imagine there becomes an unspoken understanding of their roles. The older sibling is the benevolent tyrant, projecting goodwill until he is triggered, and then his true feelings come out in unabated fury. The younger sibling is the peasant who consistently gets the short end of the stick but is somehow tethered to the painful relationship. The younger sibling complacently submits; the older stoically nods in acknowledgement. Control has been established.

As extreme as the scenario may sound, I couldn't shake the image of the older brother's outstretched arm. Even more striking was how deeply the younger felt the mere lifting of his brother's arm—it was as if his will to protest or even speak drained from his body as he abdicated once again.

As I recall what I saw that day, I feel that God has deposited truth for husbands in the story of the older sibling complex. At times, I meditate on that story to see what God would speak to my heart through it.

I can easily relate to the younger sibling in different ways. But if I stop there, I could inadvertently begin building an altar to self-pity and a victim spirit. No, I also can see myself in the older sibling, especially when it comes to marriage, my most intimate human relationship. I can see that I have been the older sibling in this story, and I have treated Katie as my younger, less-powerful sibling. I have insisted, to some degree, that our relationship revolve around and accommodate my own wounds and insecurities. I was the husband who loved and supported his wife wholeheartedly—as long as she played by my rules. When she was docile and stayed within my safe zone, then I was pleasant and supportive. But as soon as it appeared that she was surpassing me in some area, my insecurity was triggered, and I flipped from being Katie's champion and encourager to being a grouchy older brother. I sincerely wanted to be a loving and supportive husband, but my actions proved that I was insecure and hurting.

Because of the ways I've made messes in my marriage, I can identify with Adam's fallen example as a husband. But thanks to Jesus, God doesn't identify me with my mistakes. He identifies me with His Son, Jesus, and He calls me higher into Jesus' example. Thanks to Jesus, I can change. As you read through Adam's fallen example as husband, I want you to know that I wasn't stuck as a weak and insecure husband, and wherever you are in your journey, you are not stuck either.

THE FALL

In the beginning, Adam and Eve had it very good. They had a deep connection with God, a blissful shared union, and a purpose from God. This paradise life was a gift from God, and it was a direct result of their connection with Him. To remain in their grace-filled life, Adam and Eve had to abide in and honor their relationship with the Creator. As God would proclaim in ages future, "If you keep my commands, you will remain in my love" (John 15:10). Just as God loved them into being and set them apart for a purpose, they also needed to choose to love and obey Him. Their choices would be clearly seen in their treatment of God's command to Adam: "You are free to eat from any tree in the garden; but you must not eat from the tree of the knowledge of good and evil, for when you eat from it you will certainly die" (Gen. 2:16–17). Just as in marriage, God required Adam and Eve to be committed to their relationship with Him, even in the face of other options.

In Genesis 3, a new character entered the scene of God's story; he was called the serpent. He was created by God, but as the story unfolded, it became evident that the serpent was not an ally but rather an enemy of God and humanity. In time, the Author's story would reveal the serpent's true character as one who rebelled against God and now heaps accusations against God's people. This enemy came against God's relationship with His people and against marriage, which is the living metaphor of God's relationship with His bride, made up of all who trust in Jesus as their Lord and Savior.

In the Genesis account of the fall, the serpent's opposition to God came through his crafty words to Adam and Eve. He did not directly tell them to worship him instead of God. Instead, he planted doubts and accusations in their minds against God's character and goodness. He sought to usurp their authority and commission as rulers of the earth by convincing them to break their connection with God, who commissioned them. Instead of seeking overt worship from Adam and Eve, the serpent sought covert worship by getting them to forsake God's commands. The serpent taught Adam and Eve to distrust God, live independently from Him, and deify themselves. The serpent is Satan, the father of lies, who wages war against God and His bride, and his fingerprints were all over Adam's fall.

After being given a life of pure fellowship with God, Adam and Eve broke fellowship with their Creator by heeding the serpent's words instead of obeying God's commands. They used their freedom to embrace prideful independence from God. Adam's decisions have affected all of humankind, and his fallen legacy is still being perpetuated in the lives of men around the world today.

The biblical account of Adam's life gives us the profile of a fallen husband and the root issues that led to his fall. By learning from his mistakes, you can understand your own shortcomings and learn how to end ungodly patterns in your life. I encourage you to take a moment in prayer now, asking God to speak to you as you read this chapter. Ask Him to show you any way that Adam's fallen model is influencing you, and then choose to repent by turning from those ungodly patterns and submitting to His leadership in your life. That way, you will be able to not only avoid the pain and destruction resulting from Adam's model, but also take the first step towards establishing a godly legacy and heritage in your life, your family, and the world.

PRIDE

All the consequences of Adam and Eve's sin, all the death and destruction sin reaped over the ages, and all the cascading brokenness that rolled down over the generations of humankind can be traced back to the issue of pride.

Pride is related to being arrogant or disdainful. *Pride* refers to "showing one's self above others…despising others or even treating them with contempt." The New Testament uses the Greek word *hyperēphanos* to describe a *proud* person, which literally means to overshine.[1] People who are proud see themselves as more important and more valuable than the people around them; they try to be more than God directs. Pride is ugly, but it's also easy. It's so easy that Adam and Eve, who were in communion with God and had no inherited pattern of sin, found a way to sin in pride. Before there was even a third human being on the scene, Adam had already fallen into the pride of separating from God and Eve and placing himself above them.

Pride is also subtle. It's easy to overlook because it's an issue of the heart. It's internal—behind the eyes, out of reach of the hands, and unheard by one's own ears. The thought that I could even keep myself from pride is in itself prideful. Pride happens when you step out of relationship and insist on being independent. It happens when you look with disdain on those around you and choose to go it alone—that decision can be made out loud or in silence deep within your heart.

It's no mystery what inevitably happens once pride has taken root in a human heart. Proverbs tells us that "pride goes before destruction, a haughty spirit before a fall" (16:18). *The Message* version of this verse is very direct, saying, "First pride, then the crash—the bigger the ego, the harder the fall." Adam learned this the hard way.

When we first meet Adam in Genesis, pride was not something that he outwardly identified with or bragged about. The original sin did not start with him belittling Eve or telling God he wanted to be in charge, but Adam's pride presented itself when he was under pressure. The Genesis account gives the context for Adam's fallen example:

> Now the serpent was more crafty than any of the wild animals the LORD God had made. He said to the

woman, "Did God really say, 'You must not eat from any tree in the garden'?"

The woman said to the serpent, "We may eat fruit from the trees in the garden, but God did say, 'You must not eat fruit from the tree that is in the middle of the garden, and you must not touch it, or you will die.'"

"You will not certainly die," the serpent said to the woman. "For God knows that when you eat from it your eyes will be opened, and you will be like God, knowing good and evil."

When the woman saw that the fruit of the tree was good for food and pleasing to the eye, and also desirable for gaining wisdom, she took some and ate it. She also gave some to her husband, who was with her, and he ate it. Then the eyes of both of them were opened, and they realized they were naked; so they sewed fig leaves together and made coverings for themselves.

Then the man and his wife heard the sound of the Lord God as he was walking in the garden in the cool of the day, and they hid from the Lord God among the trees of the garden. But the Lord God called to the man, "Where are you?"

He answered, "I heard you in the garden, and I was afraid because I was naked; so I hid."

And he said, "Who told you that you were naked? Have you eaten from the tree that I commanded you not to eat from?"

The man said, "The woman you put here with me—she gave me some fruit from the tree, and I ate it."

Then the LORD God said to the woman, "What is this you have done?"

The woman said, "The serpent deceived me, and I ate."

—GENESIS 3:1–13

When Eve ate the forbidden fruit, Adam was with her and stood by silently—physically present but emotionally absent (Gen. 3:6). Together they strived to be more than God directed. After realizing their own nakedness, they worked together to sew fig leaves and make coverings. But when "the man and his wife heard the sound of the LORD God," they hid (Gen. 3:8). As God questioned Adam, he squirmed and shuffled before finally placing the blame on God and Eve, defending his pride. And with Adam and Eve's sin, they fell into unfathomable waves of brokenness upon brokenness that have rolled over humankind ever since.

Like lemon juice from a squeezed lemon, the pride in Adam's heart became obvious when he got squeezed by his life circumstances. He protected himself at the expense of others, and he prioritized his own safety over his connection with both God and Eve. Adam's account of his own actions was full of pride, overshining the truth, and he cast blame on both Eve and God. Adam's pride blinded him, and it cost him nearly everything.

Whenever you identify pride within yourself, it may be tempting to react the way Adam did. Adam embraced his pride by hiding—he put up a wall in his relationships, and he blamed others while minimizing his own mistakes. But this is not how to be delivered from pride; Adam's methods just take you deeper into bondage.

To deal with pride, you need to humble yourself and connect to the people around you, and you need to be in right relationship with God. After his first mistake of passivity while the serpent spoke with Eve, and then choosing to partake with Eve, Adam still refused to take responsibility. He persisted in willful stubbornness until God finally relented and gave Adam what he was so determined to have: prideful independence. This is the same banner waving over many brokenhearted and lonely people who resist authentic and vulnerable relationships with God and others—the very place that broken and lonely hearts are healed.

Adam's pride not only blinded him to his approaching fall, but it also left him painfully unaware of the destruction that would be left in the wake of his fall. His actions and words exposed his heart posture to be one of pride, self-importance, and disdain for those around him. There is much to lose if pride's cycle of destruction is left unchecked by repentance, humility, and connection. Adam's choice to embrace pride yielded unfathomable consequences for himself and for humankind.

Proverbs says that "the prudent see danger and take refuge, but the simple keep going and pay the penalty" (22:3). Pride was Adam's first step toward the exit door of paradise. It was a path that he had chosen, and sadly, he followed it to the bitter end. Yet Adam was not done building his fallen legacy. He discovered firsthand that the pride of forsaking God was far more damaging and devastating than the serpent had ever said.

INSECURITY

In addition to fostering pride, the enemy will seek to destroy relationships through insecurity and fear. When people feel insecure, they lack assurance and confidence, feeling anxious, fearful, and self-conscious instead. Someone who struggles with insecurity and fear may find it difficult to have the fortitude and consistency needed to form deeper connections. These kinds of feelings can limit your ability to trust and share yourself with others. Oftentimes, people who are under the influence of insecurity and fear end up showing the worst version of themselves to the people around them.

Looking at Adam and Eve's fall, it is easy to see that insecurity and fear were influencing them. Before the fall, the serpent's slanted questions misquoted God and injected tension into Adam and Eve's minds by pitting his words against God's. These subversive tactics were intended to bring instability, distrust, and ultimately betrayal into Adam and Eve's relationships. The serpent started by asking open-ended questions that misrepresented the Creator, asking, "Did God really say, 'You must not eat from any tree in the garden'?" (Gen. 3:1). Then the statements moved to direct accusations against God as he said to Eve, "You will certainly not die.… For God knows that when you eat from it your eyes will be opened, and you will be like God, knowing good and evil" (3:4). Instead of standing securely in their identity as God's children, Adam and Eve allowed the line of questioning to erode their trust in Him. In their insecurity, they allowed the enemy to build a case against God in their minds. It did not take long for them to forsake their commitment to God's word and to trust the serpent's voice over their Creator's voice. But insecurity and fear didn't stop there.

After Adam and Eve ate the fruit, their fears skyrocketed as the consequences of their actions came crashing in on them. They disobeyed God's commands, and then they panicked when they heard Him walking toward them! Instead of being able to stay present in their relationship with God and admit their mistakes, they went into hiding. It's clear by the end of Genesis 3 that Adam was not only insecure and afraid, but he broke connection with God and Eve because of it. God freely blessed them with purpose, authority, and favor, but at the serpent's words they leaped from the security of their relationship with God into the mirage of power presented by the enemy. Not only were the serpent's promises empty, but making decisions out of insecurity and fear cost Adam and Eve the blessings God had already secured for them.

Insecurity and fear may appear to be opposites of pride, but they are really just fruits from the same tree that exalts self above others. It is not surprising that Adam and Eve would be assaulted with feelings of insecurity and fear, for those feelings are in direct opposition to their call from God to rule the earth with authority. God was confident in His choice to appoint these two as pioneers and progenitors in the world He created, but they had to choose it. Instead of holding on to their God-given commission and identity, Adam and Eve exchanged them for an enemy-inspired view of themselves rooted in pride, insecurity, and fear.

It's worth highlighting that Adam was present with Eve during her exchanges with the serpent. Oftentimes, when this passage is discussed, Adam is not remembered as being present. That's probably because he was radio silent and emotionally absent during an incredibly important time in his marriage. The text tells us plainly, "When the woman saw…the fruit…she took some and ate it. She also gave some to her husband, who was with her, and he ate it" (Gen. 3:6). Adam had no shortage of opportunities to step in and take action. He was present when the enemy deceptively questioned Eve, he was present when Eve misquoted the commission he received directly from God, and he was present when his wife broke that command. And to top it all off, Adam threw in the towel and deliberately disobeyed God's instruction by eating the fruit himself. Adam was physically present but emotionally absent, and that became his legacy.

Adam's model as a husband is inseparably linked to passivity, apathy, and emotional absence, stemming from insecurity and fear. His silence and inaction scream for an answer, but men who are passive or emotionally detached have retreated into themselves. Instead of being present and active in the relationship, they abdicate their power and become compliant to a fault. Adam isolated himself instead of choosing to trust, to be vulnerable, and to connect with God and Eve. Because he allowed insecurity and fear in his life, Adam wasn't able to be the child of God and husband he was made to be.

The destruction in Adam's model continued as pride, insecurity, and fear built their ungodly stronghold. But the next layer of Adam's cascading fall wrought more damage as he picked up a harsh and destructive tool called self-protection.

SELF-PROTECTION

Whenever a person has difficulty connecting with others or receiving from them, self-protection can come into play. Self-protection is the way that people get their needs met when they don't trust others enough to receive from them. Oftentimes, the deepest need for someone who's self-protecting is to feel safe. If someone doesn't know how to feel protected or safe when around others, then self-protection can kick into gear as the soul's last resort to finding safety. It is rooted in a survivalist mentality and is a common coping mechanism for people living in insecurity and fear. The greater the heart's pain or fear, the more drastic measures it may take to feel safe. Just like a dog that has been wounded might attack someone trying to help, when people are in pain or afraid, their self-protective reactions can hurt the people that are closest to them.

After Adam and Eve ate the forbidden fruit, their eyes were opened and they realized the weight of their sin. Eve maintained connection with Adam when she broke God's command and offered him the fruit; they even managed to cooperate to make coverings for themselves. But when they heard God walking in the garden, Adam's demeanor toward Eve changed. At the sound of God's footsteps, Adam's insecurity and fear drove him to self-protect like a wounded animal, and everyone around him suffered.

As God started the conversation, Adam acknowledged, "I heard you in the garden, and I was afraid because I was naked; so I hid" (Gen. 3:10). The Lord probed further: "Who told you that you were naked? Have you eaten from the tree that I commanded you not to eat from?" (v. 11). But Adam refused to give a direct answer, and he did not take personal responsibility. He winced at God's inquiry and immediately began dishing out blame to anyone in the vicinity. "The woman you put here with me—she gave me some fruit from the tree…" I envision Adam's voice trailing off as he finally acknowledged under his breath, "And I ate it" (v. 12). I can imagine Eve's shock at the change that took place in Adam—he stood by her without saying a word when she ate the fruit, but now he was conveniently placing the weight of their sin back on her!

Just a few verses earlier, Adam's heart overflowed with joy and profound awe at the sight of his wife. But now, out of his mouth flowed blame and accusations against her. Instead of laying down his life for Eve, Adam was actively sacrificing his connection with her for the sake of his own safety and protection.

Adam could have chosen to take personal responsibility for his sins of disobedience and passivity. He could have chosen loyalty to God and Eve instead of betraying their trust. He could have protected his connections with God and with Eve instead of breaking away. But Adam did not choose these things. His heart posture of pride, insecurity, and fear pushed him to self-protect while refusing to give account for his own actions. Adam betrayed the trust of those closest to him, and his choices damaged their connection.

Adam's legacy was formed by his choices, and the evidence of his fallen legacy was seen in his children—specifically in the life of his son Cain. In anger, Cain murdered his brother, Abel. After he committed this sin, God came to Cain, just as he did to Adam, and asked him, "Where is your brother Abel?" But Cain brazenly responded, "I don't know.…Am I my brother's keeper?" (Gen. 4:9). Just as Adam did, Cain self-protected in his moment of decision by refusing to take personal responsibility for his actions. Instead, he deflected the attention from himself and questioned God. Cain followed Adam's fallen model and perpetuated his fallen legacy.

Self-protection can present in many different ways, but generally speaking, those who use this unhealthy tool place a higher value on their sense of safety than on other people. They act to ensure their safety, even at the expense or pain of others. One way that self-protection can be seen in the lives of men is through the use of "fight" tools with their wives. These tools are aggressive, assertive, and actively destructive, and they include rage, anger, blaming others, accusing others, hatred, bitterness, abuse (physical, sexual, verbal, emotional, etc.), intimidation, throwing things, and other similar behaviors. These things are the fruit of Adam's model taking root in a man's life, and they are unacceptable for a man who follows Jesus.

Self-protection can also present through "flight" tools such as withdrawal, isolation, the silent treatment, or other kinds of passive manipulation in which the husband emotionally goes away. With these tools it is very easy to falsely claim innocence and to blame someone else, justifying yourself as you slyly ask, "What did I do wrong?" But this kind of self-protection causes damage through an active absence of communication, emotional presence, and/or love. For someone on the receiving end of this kind of manipulative behavior, the experience is different than the aggressive "fight" tools, but the pain is just as real. Other "flight" tools of self-protection include workaholism, busyness, pornography, alcoholism, and other addictive behaviors.

These are just a few of the fruits coming from the root of pride, insecurity, and self-protection. They may be familiar to you, but don't believe the lies that these things are harmless, that no one is impacted by them, and that they won't damage you, your spouse, your marriage, and your family. Even if it is familiar, the tool of self-protection is destructive, and it's used by the enemy to perpetuate Adam's fallen model.

SECRECY

Survival is the goal of a man on the run from God and his spouse, and the next survival tool that Adam picked up was secrecy. Secrecy provides protection for people who are afraid and ashamed. It affords them a degree of hiddenness without requiring them to admit their mistakes or change. But a proud man doesn't realize that by entertaining secrecy, he is befriending foolishness. As Proverbs states:

> There is a spirit named Foolish....She preaches to all who walk by her who are clueless to what is happening: "Come home with me." She invites those who are easily led astray, saying, "Illicit sex is the best sex of all. Our secret affair will be sweeter than all others." Little do they know when they answer her call that she dwells among the spirits of the dead, and all her guests soon become citizens of hell!
>
> —Proverbs 9:13, 15–18, tpt

When they were in fellowship with God, Adam and Eve were both naked and unashamed (Gen. 2:25). They were clothed with the light of God and lived in pure and unbroken fellowship with Him. But after the fall, they became keenly aware of their nakedness, and they began to hide themselves with shame, fear, and secrecy as their coverings.

Shame is a mirror that tells you that you don't *have* a problem, but rather you *are* the problem. But you can't scrape your skin hard enough to get rid of shame—it runs too deep. For men following Adam's model, the only way to keep from being embarrassed or ashamed is by hiding. Surrendering to the voice of shame, you hide your true self so others won't see it, convinced it is ugly and repulsive. When you surrender to shame, you believe your real self will be rejected by others if it is allowed to see the light of day. This shame leads to secrecy that can take various forms. To keep your secrets safe, you may run away, minimize your mistakes, or even deny you made any mistakes. You may even hide in plain sight by projecting a false version of yourself to the world, while working overtime to keep your secrets under wraps.

Secrecy often starts with hiding something small. Like the first step down a slippery slope, it's easy to justify a little bit of secrecy and not realize that the door of destruction is being opened: just one website; just one conversation; just one last drink; just one more glance. But that "just one" is the first step on a path ending in moral failure, a broken home, and ruined relationships. After taking the first step, you may never look back, and your pride can blind you to the fact that you're quickly sliding down a slippery slope into deeper and darker depths of secret sin.

With private web browsing, internet anonymity, and the world at our fingertips, the temptation to entertain ungodly secrecy is real. The serpent is still prodding us to doubt God's goodness, offering a quick fix to meet a need God's already provided for. The fruit looks different in people's lives, but it's all from the same forbidden tree. For some, it's gambling or pornography; for others, it's alcohol or drugs; for still others, it's adultery through sexual intimacy or the more socially acceptable emotional adultery. For some reading this, you don't struggle with any of those things, but there's still an area of your life that you won't let your wife into, an area of you that is secret and off-limits to her. Whether in seed form or fully matured, secrecy and concealed sin is a hallmark of Adam's example.

Instead of running to God with his pain and fear, Adam allowed his guilty conscience to lead him away from God and into hiding. He finally spoke to God after God came to him and initiated the conversation. Only then did Adam authentically acknowledge, "I was afraid because I was naked; so I hid" (Gen. 3:10).

It's all too easy to justify a life of secrecy and sin, especially if you're feeling emotions such as fear, loneliness, shame, hurt, or exhaustion. But secrecy is lethal to relationships, and if it is entertained, it can become the breeding ground for betrayal, addiction, and other sins. It's better to repent now than to persist in pride.

> Whoever conceals their sins does not prosper, but the one who confesses and renounces them finds mercy.
>
> —Proverbs 28:13

For those practicing Adam's fallen model, there's an invitation to forsake it and receive mercy before reaping the consequences for Adam's sin, which are wrapped up in one chilling word: *separation*.

SEPARATION

Finally, for men persisting in Adam's fallen model, the progression of brokenness comes to summation in the breakdown of relationships. This brokenness manifests in physical, emotional, and spiritual separation. In Genesis 3, God responded to the choices made by the serpent, Adam, and Eve, and He pronounced the consequences for each of their actions.

> So the Lord God said to the serpent, "Because you have done this, cursed are you above all livestock and all wild animals! You will crawl on your belly and you will eat dust all the days of your life. And I will put enmity between you and the woman, and between your offspring and hers; he will crush your head, and you will strike his heel."

> To the woman he said, "I will make your pains in childbearing very severe; with painful labor you will give birth to children. Your desire will be for your husband, and he will rule over you."
>
> To Adam he said, "Because you listened to your wife and ate fruit from the tree about which I commanded you, 'You must not eat from it,' cursed is the ground because of you; through painful toil you will eat food from it all the days of your life. It will produce thorns and thistles for you, and you will eat the plants of the field. By the sweat of your brow you will eat your food until you return to the ground, since from it you were taken; for dust you are and to dust you will return."
>
> —Genesis 3:14–19

Adam's model began with the subtle sin of pride, but it ended with drastic consequences, including broken relationships and separation. Adam's world came crashing down on him as he reaped the fruit of what he sowed. This separation was not the pronouncement of a cruel God looking for ways to punish His children. It was actually the result of choices that His children made using the freedom He gave them. Adam used his freedom to choose separation in his relationships with God and Eve, and he received the consequences of his choices. The freedom to choose or refuse love is essential for love to exist, because love cannot be demanded—it must be chosen.

In Romans 1, Paul taught us about how God addressed Adam and Eve's sin without violating their freedom: He gave them what they wanted. According to this passage, when people persist in using their freedom to choose godlessness and wickedness, God gives them over to their own sinful desires. One Bible version says, "God lifted off his restraining hand and let them have full expression of their sinful and shameful desires" (Rom. 1:24, TPT). The Greek word for *lifted off* means to surrender, to hand over, to give or deliver over, and to commit.[2]

God values your freedom and your relationship with Him so much that He is willing to give you your desires, even when they violate your connection with Him. It's a scary reality, but it can also be seen in the Genesis 3 passage for both Adam and Eve.

To Eve, God said, "Your desire will be for your husband, and he will rule over you" (Gen. 3:16). In the beginning, Eve was created out of Adam's side, and they were given a side-by-side commission to rule the earth. God's pronouncement over Eve in Genesis was a change from His original design. The change came because Eve chose to come under the ungodly leadership and earthly wisdom of the serpent instead of standing in her God-given assignment. In place of partnership with her husband, Eve received a relational dynamic of inferiority and her husband ruling over her. God gave her over to her choice to forsake God's empowering leadership and to come under the slavery of the serpent's leadership. Her decision was one of separation, loss of side-by-side connection, and a new dynamic with Adam that looked more like subjection than shared leadership.

God also made a pronouncement over Adam, saying that the ground would be cursed, that Adam would toil painfully to yield a harvest, and that he would return to the dust of the ground. All this, God said to Adam, was "because you listened to your wife and ate fruit from the tree about which I commanded you, 'You must not eat from it'" (Gen. 3:17). In Adam's notorious moment of silence and passivity, he resisted God's commands and distanced himself from both God and his wife. Instead of leaning into his relationships and becoming vulnerable, he chose separation. God handed Adam over to the isolation and aloneness that he chose, and that separation would be bitter, ending in death and a return to the dust of the earth. Dust was the exact substance of who Adam was without God. Adam had forsaken his Creator, and now God, who loved him into existence and placed him in paradise, was giving Adam over to his choice to be without his Creator. He would again become dust, void of the aliveness that comes from connection and fellowship with God (Gen. 3:17–19).

After God finished pronouncing the consequences of Adam and Eve's decisions, He compassionately made coverings for Adam and Eve before they were escorted out of the garden.

> The LORD God made garments of skin for Adam and his wife and clothed them. And the LORD God said, "The man has now become like one of us, knowing good and evil. He must not be allowed to reach out his hand and take also from the tree of life and eat, and live forever." So the LORD God banished him from the Garden of Eden to work the ground from which he had been taken. After he drove the man out, he placed on the east side of the Garden of Eden cherubim and a flaming sword flashing back and forth to guard the way to the tree of life.
>
> —Genesis 3:21–24

Adam and Eve's intimate communion with God was broken, and the way back to their place of fellowship was now blocked by heavenly beings, swords, and fire. For Adam, the consequences of his pride, insecurity, self-protection, and secrecy were separation from God, separation from his wife, separation from his home, and finally, separation from his own life through death.

A SEED OF HOPE

Adam is famous for his sin, but after looking at his mistakes, you may realize you have more in common with his fallen model than you thought. It can be hard to admit, but in many ways Adam has been our broken father, and we have been his broken sons.

Yet, even in the narrative of the fall, there is a Seed of hope. As Romans 5 says, "Adam, who got us into this, also points ahead to the One who will get us out of it" (v. 14, MSG). The One who is to come is the same Seed of the woman whom God spoke about in Genesis 3—He who will crush the head of the serpent (v. 15). And for husbands who choose it, there is a Seed of hope available to them, regardless of personal circumstances or history.

I also want to acknowledge that Adam was more than his sin. He was the honored progenitor of humankind, the same race our Lord died to save. After taking this chapter to learn from Adam's mistakes, I also want to honor him as our very-great-grandfather and one of God's children.

I think we honor Adam best by valuing him as a person and refusing to replicate his mistakes. The attributes of pride, insecurity, self-protection, secrecy, and separation are an ungodly inheritance for husbands. This is a default family pattern and ungodly family tradition that has been handed down over many generations. This is the pattern that you and I are called and privileged to break in our generation and for those coming after us.

I want to challenge you to fiercely resist Adam's model in your marriages and families. Prayerfully consider how these attributes may be present in your own life and what it will take to cut them off (Matt. 5:30). (See the prayer guide at the end of this book.) These cycles need to be broken, and thanks to Jesus, they can be broken in your life. Through His life and death, Jesus opened the way for a new kind of husband who not only leaves a godly legacy but also experiences marriage as God intended it from the beginning, not in its fallen state.

REFLECTION QUESTIONS

- What are the main characteristics of Adam's fallen model as a husband?
- Do you identify with any of those characteristics? How so?
- What concepts in this chapter resonated with you the most?

CHAPTER 3

Joseph: The Humility of a Husband

> So Joseph also went up from the town of Nazareth in Galilee to Judea, to Bethlehem the town of David, because he belonged to the house and line of David. He went there to register with Mary, who was pledged to be married to him and was expecting a child.
> —Luke 2:4–5

It was our first Christmas as a married couple. After finishing college in Philadelphia, Katie and I got married and started our new life in Del Ray, a neighborhood outside of Washington, DC. We moved into a tiny apartment that took up the third floor of a home on a residential street. The apartment was the top floor of the house, so our ceiling slanted downward in line with the house's angled roof. The ceilings dipped so low that you couldn't stand upright at the edges of the apartment. We stuffed couches, stools, and anything else we could find against the walls of the room to make use of our limited space—and to protect visitors from banging their heads on the low ceiling.

As Katie and I explored our new life together, our hearts were full. We were thrilled by all of the new firsts of our first year of marriage, not the least being our first Christmas tree. Its humility was astounding: this tree had to fit up two flights of stairs and through our tiny apartment door and then be able to stand upright in our apartment without poking the slanted ceilings. Despite the drama, or maybe because of it, we loved our tiny little tree. We decorated it, then sat back and enjoyed the beauty of Christmas and the gracious gift God gave us in the double joy of a shared life.

Although I was overflowing with gratitude, tender love, and wonder, at that time in my life, I honestly was not good at holidays, celebration, or even joy. I was following Katie's lead on the Christmas celebration front and loving it. She was constantly decorating, cooking, celebrating Jesus, lighting scented candles, and being the love-gushing superhuman that she is. I loved her, and I loved our life together.

When Christmas Day finally arrived, the two of us sat down and exchanged gifts. I honestly don't remember much about the gifts we gave each other that year, but there is one detail that is still sharp in my mind—a Christmas card I received from Katie, which she attached to one of my gifts. That card impacted me deeply, and it still does to this day.

Before I opened the gift, I opened the envelope and removed the card. As I did, I saw a traditional Christmas card with a painted portrait of Mary and Joseph looking at the newborn Jesus, lying in the manger between them. As I looked closer, I felt an aliveness resting on it that was resonating with the Spirit alive within me. Something about that Christmas card's illustration was pulling at me. I felt as though God was nudging me to look deeper and discover a hidden treasure He placed there for me.

On our first Christmas as a married couple, I meditated on the image of that wonder-filled couple, and I noted what I perceived. I saw that Mary and Joseph had a special marriage and a joint assignment from God. I saw a God-blessed marriage that did not revolve around the husband. I saw that the wife was actually visible because she was not relegated to the shadowy space behind her husband. I saw that the wife was honored for who she was, not for what man she was in relationship with. Yes, I could see two people who together leaped into an incredible God adventure with both feet, and they deeply experienced life and love through both sorrow and glory.

As I write this chapter today, it has been years since that first Christmas. Yet, when I bring that simple card to remembrance, I feel a tender burning in my heart that pulsates with the light and life of the Spirit. It's the same light and life that I saw resting on the portrait of Mary and Joseph.

God is not done with marriage. It is a gift to humankind and a revelation of His heart toward us. Joseph and Mary are part of that revelation, and I'm honored and pleased for us to journey through their lives together.

MEET JOSEPH

The Bible doesn't give much detail about Joseph. We know he was the husband of Mary and the earthly father of Jesus, and we even know he worked as a carpenter. But beyond those basic facts, we don't have many specifics about him as an individual.

Actually, when I read through the Gospels, it seems like Joseph's life was mentioned in order to point us to Mary and God's redemptive plan being unveiled through her. The dearth of detail on Joseph's life speaks volumes for those who are listening.

Even though Joseph doesn't get much attention in the Gospels, we know that God placed him in the exact time and space that he lived (Acts 17:26). Out of the billions of people to be born over thousands of years, God intentionally chose one man, Joseph, to be Mary's husband and Jesus' adoptive father.

Through Joseph and Mary's story, God revealed His heart to restore what humankind lost at the fall. And specifically for men, God provided a redemptive response to Adam's fallen example through the life of Joseph, the husband of Mary. His example also set the stage for Jesus the Bridegroom and His example to us.

Joseph's model is made up of four attributes that can be clearly seen in his life. Through these attributes, his life exemplified what it can look like to be a godly husband. The first of these attributes is the antithesis of Adam's model and the foundation of Joseph's; it is the virtue of humility.

EMBRACING HUMILITY

Humility comes from the Latin word *humilitatem,* which means "lowness, small stature; insignificance." Literally it means "on the ground," from the root word *humus,* meaning "earth."[1] Though Adam was made from the soil of the earth, it resisted him after the fall. Joseph, however, resisted Adam's model and embraced humility—along with all of its plain, earthy substance.

Jesus' earthly father was first introduced through a genealogy in Matthew 1. Going back in time, Matthew recounted Joseph's lineage and how the humble carpenter was a direct descendant of some noteworthy and influential Jewish leaders: Abraham, the father of the faith; Isaac; Jacob, who, God himself renamed Israel; King David; and King Solomon. But I wonder how Joseph felt about his ancestry.

On the one hand, I imagine he was proud to have such a rich heritage in his own family tree. Just consider King David—he is a hero of the Jewish people and his radical exploits with God are still talked about to this day.

But on the other hand, that same national pride and honored family history was a stark contrast to the faded glory of the daily life of Joseph and his people. Unlike the glory days of David's kingship, in Joseph's day the Jewish people were ruled by another nation: the brutal Roman Empire. This empire was known for conquering entire nations and bringing them under its control. Joseph was not recognized as royalty or a decorated warrior, but instead, he was a humbled carpenter, who, along with his nation, was under the thumb of Roman oppressors.

Considering Joseph's life, I wonder if his rich family history became a heavy burden. I wonder if his royal identity became a liability in the shadow of the Roman centurions who rode into his village with horse and chariot. Maybe it was safer for Joseph to conceal his royal identity. If he would just become a docile, submissive guy and blend in with the crowd, maybe there wouldn't be any trouble for him and his family under the yoke of the Roman government. The weight of his family's glorious past may have felt more like mockery. What was meant for honor had been turned and twisted into a crown of thorns, just as when Pilate nailed the sign above Jesus' head on the cross, proclaiming, "THIS IS JESUS, THE KING OF THE JEWS" (Matt. 27:37).

I wonder how Joseph would have responded if he heard Matthew reciting his dynamic genealogy. Perhaps he would have stood at attention in respect and pride, lifting his head and squaring his shoulders. Or maybe he would have buried his head in grief at its disappointing contrasts with the humble state of his life and nation.

Though aspects of Joseph's life may have felt humiliating, walking in true humility is always a choice. Through various contradictions and disappointments Joseph chose humility and refused to embrace Adam's model of pride and separation. God used Joseph's humbleness of heart and brought him into the fold of His redemptive plan.

Joseph's humility can be seen throughout the Gospel narrative, but one of the most powerful ways was through the fear of God and his subsequent obedience and submission to God's leading. As Proverbs says, "Humility is the fear of the Lord; its wages are riches and honor and life" (22:4). Joseph's fear of God and submission to His leading is the second attribute of his model as a godly husband.

SUBMITTING TO GOD

Matthew describes Joseph as "faithful to the law" (Matt. 1:19), or "a righteous man" (NASB), and the short biblical account of his life gives us multiple examples of that faithfulness.

After Mary gave birth to the newborn Jesus, Joseph and Mary went through the God-ordained processes described in the Law. Luke 2 plainly states that they did "everything required by the Law of the Lord" (v. 39). This included circumcision of the newborn boy, purification rites, offering a sacrifice of a pair of doves or two young pigeons, and presenting the baby to God. Their lives were devoted to God, and even when Jesus was a child, "every year Jesus' parents went to Jerusalem for the Festival of the Passover" (v. 41). They were devout Jews who faithfully fulfilled their obligations to God's Law.

But Joseph's faithfulness to God went beyond external actions, beyond outward appearances, and beyond doing only what the religious culture of his day would approve of. Joseph's righteousness emanated from his heart. He was sensitive to the Spirit of God and reverently responsive to His leadings. Even when God's leading was contrary to social norms and put his personal safety at risk, Joseph responded faithfully. His responses to the unexpected and trying circumstances in his life show us that not only was he obedient to the Law, but his heart was fully submitted to God. His decisions in the Gospels show this clearly.

To start, Joseph discovered that his fiancée was pregnant before they slept together, only to have his perplexity compounded by Mary claiming the pregnancy happened "through the Holy Spirit" (Matt. 1:18). It was an out-of-this-world claim, and I'm guessing that Joseph was incredulous. I can imagine him trying to understand the situation and asking himself, "Even if what she said is true, why didn't the angel come to me first?" I don't know Joseph's upbringing, but it could have been outside of his paradigm that God would send an angel to a woman ahead of her fiancé, who was a devout Jewish man. After all, even the New Testament calls him righteous!

To say the least, Joseph found himself in an unusual circumstance. I can imagine him trying to understand his options. On the one hand, it looked as if Mary lied to him, betrayed his trust, and was unfaithful to him. On the other hand, if she was telling the truth, God had not yet clued him in with the same encounter or clarity that Mary apparently had. In reality, the truth was much stranger than what Joseph could imagine: God was calling him to become the adoptive father of the Son of God, the Messiah, whose mother was a virgin.

When compared with Adam, Joseph's life has some interesting parallels. Before God created Eve, He gave instructions to Adam not to eat the forbidden fruit. When Adam and Eve disobeyed God's word and ate the fruit, Adam pridefully separated from Eve. With Joseph and Mary, God deposited His Word within the woman before the man was aware, and because of the circumstances, Mary's pregnancy appeared to be the result of sin. Joseph had a decision to make. Would he be like Adam, the man who pridefully separated himself from the woman? Or would he humbly cover her supposed disgrace and draw near?

God helped Joseph by speaking to him in a dream. In the dream, an angel confirmed what Mary said to Joseph: "Joseph son of David, do not be afraid to take Mary home as your wife, because what is conceived in her is from the Holy Spirit" (Matt. 1:20). If Joseph were a proud man, then even an angelic encounter may not have convinced him to change his plan to divorce Mary. But "when Joseph woke up, he did what the angel of the Lord had commanded him and took Mary home as his wife" (v. 24).

When I read the Gospels, Joseph seems to have had a heart of mercy toward Mary, even after he found out she was pregnant. I wonder if God delighted in Joseph's slowness to distance himself from Mary and his hesitance to expose her to public disgrace. On a deeper level, I also wonder if God delights in husbands who have a heart of mercy toward their wives, intentionally affirm the dignity and value of their wives, and refuse to shame, belittle, or embarrass them, even if it feels justified. I believe God delights in men who submit to Him and are secure enough to love relentlessly, even when they feel lied to, used, or betrayed.

Joseph was reverently responsive to what God spoke, and he promptly carried out God's supernatural guidance. In Isaiah 66, God said that He esteems those who are "humble and contrite in spirit, and who tremble at [His] word" (v. 2). Because of Joseph's response to God's leadership, I believe he was one whom God esteems.

Joseph's heart was submitted to God. That submission enabled him to obey the angel's instructions, to repent of his plan to divorce Mary, and to fully embrace his marriage to Mary—for which he would be misunderstood, ostracized, and judged by his community. His humble resolve continued to manifest throughout his brief appearance in the Gospel story. An angel repeatedly appeared to Joseph, and each time he reverently responded to the direction from the Lord (e.g., Matt. 2:13). By doing so, he helped fulfill the God-ordained commission given to him and his wife.

IDENTIFYING AS A HUSBAND

One day I was reading Matthew 1, and I almost fell out of my chair. Verse 16 leaped off the page and slapped my preconceived notions in their ignorant face. I was raised in the church, and I have read the Bible my whole life, but I never saw this before. The surprising verse was at the end of that chapter's genealogy section. My attention was arrested when Matthew ended the genealogy of Jesus by referencing "*Joseph, the husband of Mary*, and Mary was the mother of Jesus who is called the Messiah" (Matt. 1:16, emphasis added). I was shocked by what I was seeing in this unassuming and generally ignored passage of Scripture, and the implications sent me reeling: Joseph is the only person in the genealogy to be identified as a *husband*.

Biblical genealogies are typically based on the identity of the man alone, without mention of women. The genealogy in Matthew 1 is similar, with its abundance of male references and descriptions of who is whose father or son. There are only four women mentioned by name in the generations listed: Tamar, Rahab, Ruth, and Mary. The first three are listed in reference to their male offspring—for example, Ruth, the "mother of Obed" (Matt. 1:5, GW). Based on the way that biblical genealogies were written, I would expect a similar pattern for Joseph and Mary. This would mean that the author's attention would be placed solely on the man Joseph, and whenever Joseph was mentioned, it would be primarily about his connection to other men. For Mary, this would mean she wouldn't be mentioned in the genealogy at all, or if she was, it would only be in reference to a man in her life (for example, "Mary, the mother of Jesus"), just as was done with Tamar, Rahab, and Ruth. But Matthew's head-turning description of "Joseph, the husband of Mary" didn't omit Mary, nor did it treat her as optional; it included Mary and placed a high value on the relationship of man and woman, husband and wife. Matthew introduced Joseph as the husband of Mary and thus established Joseph's role as husband as one of utmost importance in his life. Instead of a man's identity and value being found merely in the context of other men, Matthew placed Joseph's role as husband to his wife at the center of his identity and calling.

Matthew's reference to "Joseph, the husband of Mary" is significant because in the first chapter of the first book of the New Testament, the first mention and original context for the life of Joseph is in the role of husband. In direct opposition to Adam's model of separation, Joseph's biblical personhood and his very identity was inseparably linked to his wife. By listing Joseph and Mary together, Matthew emphasizes their shared identity. This identity would be tried and tested through their journey together, but Joseph would consistently and increasingly resist the aloneness of Adam's model, and he would resolutely choose to identify as Mary's husband.

To place Matthew's statement in context, I want to highlight the culture of Joseph's day. When Jesus was going throughout Galilee and Judea, teaching, healing, and proclaiming the good news, some religious leaders questioned Jesus about divorce. They asked Him, "Is it lawful for a man to divorce his wife for any and every reason?" (Matt. 19:3). Their line of questioning reveals that they wanted to perpetuate Adam's model of separation, in which powerful men separate from and disempower women. In response Jesus said:

> Haven't you read…that at the beginning the Creator "made them male and female," and said, "For this reason a man will leave his father and mother and be united to his wife, and the two will become one flesh"? So they are no longer two, but one flesh. Therefore what God has joined together, let no one separate.
>
> —MATTHEW 19:4–6

Even though the religious community of Joseph's day defended and condoned Adam's model of separation, the Creator did not. Instead, He reiterated His own design and intent from the beginning: the man would leave his father and mother and then be united to his wife, and in this marriage relationship they would have a shared identity of husband and wife.

Joseph was walking out this created design in his relationship with Mary, but the act of leaving his father and mother meant much more than just moving out of their house. That's because in Joseph's culture, a man's identity in society was directly connected to his family relationships. Joseph's tribe, his community, his occupation, and even his physical home were all connected to his family relationships. And while these aspects of his identity had a place in his married life—and rightly so—his role as husband was a central aspect of his identity that impacted all of the others.

Given the situation Joseph found himself in, it was no small decision for him to leave his father and mother's house to become Mary's husband. Her unexpected pregnancy, strange explanation, and seeming infidelity made him question the wisdom of continuing forward with their marriage plans. But because of Joseph's humility and submission to God, he was able to find the way forward, even in the face of trying circumstances. After Joseph had considered divorcing Mary, he had the following experience:

> An angel of the Lord appeared to him in a dream and said, "Joseph son of David, do not be afraid to take Mary home as your wife, because what is conceived in her is from the Holy Spirit. She will give birth to a son, and you are to give him the name Jesus, because he will save his people from their sins."...When Joseph woke up, he did what the angel of the Lord had commanded him and took Mary home as his wife. But he did not consummate their marriage until she gave birth to a son. And he gave him the name Jesus.
>
> —MATTHEW 1:20–21, 24–25

Joseph reverently responded to God's leading, even at great personal cost. By choosing to step into his identity as the husband of

Mary, Joseph accepted that he could be misunderstood or rejected by his community; he even chose sexual abstinence within his marriage for a time.

When a man decides to leave his father and mother's house and becomes one with his wife, he is redefined at a foundational level (Matt. 19:6). Men cannot afford to lose sight of this. Once a man is married, his premarriage life goes into the grave, and he comes into his new life as a husband who is joined to his wife—and he needs to reintroduce himself with his new identity to those around him. Mom and dad, brothers and sisters, work and play, hobbies and friends—every area of his life needs to receive the announcement of his new life as the husband to his wife. He is not only in relationship with her; he is *one* with her. He is not only committed to her; he *identifies* with her. He is not just a married man; he is *her* man, the husband of a specific woman. He is a new man, and he is united with her. He must not let anything bring separation to their shared identity, which God Himself joined together. He is the husband of his wife, and he must know it in his heart.

What you believe about yourself impacts your thoughts, feelings, and actions, so a married man must have his role as husband to his wife settled deeply in his heart. It is a core aspect of his identity that impacts every area of his life. As Proverbs says, "For as he thinks within himself, so is he" (23:7, TPT). By renewing your mind to the fact that you are a husband, your thoughts, feelings, and actions will begin to naturally reflect love for your wife and value for your marriage. It will also spare you the exhausting work of trying to control and micromanage your thought life, emotional urges, and behaviors when your soul is still bent toward an old, single life.

For married men who feel stuck in sinful patterns and urges, it's both tormenting and exhausting to try to control their ungodly thoughts, feelings, and actions. Without their hearts healed and minds renewed, their time, energy, and attention are focused on avoiding relational messes instead of pursuing a love relationship with their wives. It's much better to yield to the transforming work of the Spirit in your life and allow Him to transform you from the inside out. (See the prayer guide at the end of this book to learn more about this process.) When God heals you on the inside, and when you renew your mind with His truth, then your heart can be at peace because godly thoughts, feelings, and behaviors become a natural and authentic expression of who you are. A central aspect of this work of the Spirit in a married man is renewing his mind to the truth of his identity as the husband of his wife.

The enemy attacks men in this area by offering them the compromised identity of a "married bachelor." This identity justifies keeping their old selves alive on life support, while refusing to fully embrace their identities as husbands. But this reflects Adam's fallen model, and it is a far cry from God's call for husbands. A man who allows the old bachelor identity to continue into marriage will find himself out of step with his wife and with God's plan for his life. This cognitive dissonance blinds him to his purpose and call from God that are wrapped up in his identity as husband to his wife.

A man who doesn't keep a strong hold on his role and identity as a husband is not only in danger of neglecting his vows, but his complacency and disconnection can open the door to great destruction to his wife, his marriage, his family, and his life. The enemy seeks to convince men that the exclusivity of their marriages cheats them of what they could have and that they deserve more. Just as the enemy convinced Adam and Eve to eat the fruit to obtain something they already had, the enemy tells husbands that the grass is greener on the other side, and they are justified in stepping outside of their identity as a husband to get their needs met. Proverbs describes this tactic of the enemy through the lens of seduction:

> The lips of a seductress seem sweet like honey, and her smooth words are like music in your ears. But I promise you this: in the end all you'll be left with is a bitter conscience. For the sting of your sin will pierce your soul like a sword. She will ruin your life, drag you down to death, and lead you straight to hell. She has prevented many from considering the paths of life. Yes, she will take you with her where you don't want to go, sliding down a slippery road and not even realizing where the two of you will end up! Listen to me, young men, and don't forget this one thing I'm telling you—run away from her as fast as you can!
>
> —PROVERBS 5:3–7, TPT

By entertaining this seduction from the enemy, men dissociate from their identities as husbands and reap destruction and remorse. "Truth will protect you from immorality" (Prov. 6:24, TPT), but the man who isn't established in this truth of his identity as a husband is vulnerable to the enemy's schemes against his marriage. Proverbs describes these men who succumbed to seduction as being carried away "as hostages—kidnapped captives robbed of destiny" (5:23, TPT). Married men who refuse to embrace their identities as husbands open the door to the enemy's plans for their lives and neglect their God-given destinies. Proverbs describes their approaching lament: "If only I had listened to wisdom's voice and not stubbornly demanded my own way, because my heart hated to be told what to do!" (5:12, TPT).

This kind of sin can present in many different ways. Sometimes it presents as adultery through a sexual relationship outside of marriage or through pornography, but it can also present through a more subtle betrayal of emotional adultery, when a husband shares his heart with another in a way he should only share with his wife. Whatever the case, these violations of the marriage covenant start within a man's heart, impacting his thoughts, feelings, and actions. It does not always begin as an intentional act, but when a man refuses to take hold of his identity as a husband, he throws open the door to thoughts, feelings, and actions that violate both this central aspect of his identity and his marriage covenant with his wife.

The voice of wisdom in Proverbs tells men to run away from seduction as fast as they can. Don't entertain it. Don't maintain a "safe" distance by taking a few steps back. Don't decide to "just be friends" with threats to your marriage. Wisdom says run!

Wisdom is connected to submission to God and the fear of the Lord (Prov. 9:10), so the place for husbands to run is into the fear of the Lord. For husbands, this means nurturing a holy reverence for the One before whom you made your vows to your wife, the One who joined you and your wife together for no man to separate, and the One who transformed your identity from being a lone male to being a husband.

The choice to identify as a husband is one of exclusivity and severity: "My son, share your love with your wife alone. Drink from her well of pleasure and from no other" (Prov. 5:15, TPT). When a man embraces his identity as a husband, he is placing the nails in the coffin of his old, single life and of any sense of entitlement to have his sexual desires or deepest human emotional needs met outside of his relationship with his wife.

Taking hold of the truth of being a one-woman man will preemptively address many other issues. Your yes to one woman in marriage is an unequivocal no to all others. By identifying as a husband to your wife, you are declaring your yes to her, which is at the same time a resounding no to all relationships, conversations, glances, thoughts, websites, behaviors, or other things that violate your yes to your wife. On his wedding day, a man makes his vows to one woman. And from that day forward, she is his most intimate soul tie, she is his closest emotional connection, and she is his only place for sexual relations or thoughts. They belong to each other, and he identifies with her.

Joseph's decision to identify as Mary's husband came in sharp contrast to Adam's model. Instead of self-protecting, hiding in secrecy, and separating from his wife the way Adam did during hardship, Joseph drew closer to Mary. Not only did his humility and submission to God enable him to identify as Mary's husband, but they also protected him from the many traps the enemy sets for husbands. At each and every decision point in their relational journey, Joseph prioritized his connection and shared identity with Mary. Joseph accepted his identity as Mary's husband, and by doing so, he stepped wholeheartedly into his marriage with her and their God-given assignment and purpose.

The first truth of Matthew's introduction of Joseph and Mary is profound: the identity of this "son of David" is not wrapped up only in his connection to his fathers. Instead, Matthew introduces "Joseph, the husband of Mary" as primarily a married man, defined by his relationship to his wife. And within this same verse is another startling truth that takes the countercultural nature of Joseph's identity to another level.

SERVING HIS WIFE

Matthew's mention of Joseph as "the husband of Mary" not only emphasizes his role as her husband, but it positions him to serve his wife instead of having her serve him only. The placement of Joseph and Mary's names in this verse highlight Mary, not Joseph. In the previous verses, women were not listed with the men, except for Tamar, Rahab, and Ruth, who were mentioned in reference to their sons. But Mary was mentioned by name, and her husband was listed in reference to *her*. This is significant because Joseph's relationship with Mary made room for connection and side-by-side relating—but then it went deeper still. Joseph's life and legacy prove that in great humility, submission to God, and identifying as Mary's husband, Joseph positioned himself to honor, prefer, and serve Mary. This dynamic of Joseph serving Mary became a theme for their marriage and for Joseph's life.

When the realization that Joseph was positioned to serve Mary first dawned on me, I was astonished, perplexed, and embarrassed all at the same time. As I tried to internalize this subtle yet monumental shift, I felt my Bible scraping against the grain of my privileged paradigm. It was revealing my apathy, disrupting my complacency, and exposing my subconscious sense of privilege as a male Christian. In Matthew 1, God's story flipped my Adamic paradigm on its head. My maleness had blinded me to the fact that I was a participant in Adam's model by default, and in order to return to God's original intent, I couldn't just invite women into an Adamic system, built on man ruling over woman. As a child of God, as a brother to my sisters, and as a husband to my wife, I have a greater responsibility. That responsibility is to pursue God's intended commission for my marriage by shedding the Adamic power afforded to me by my culture and picking up the opposite of privilege and entitlement—by becoming a servant. Instead of trying to convert the old man and his model, they both must be put to death and left in the grave for new life to emerge. And as a man who inherited Adam's model, that means I too must be put to death, along with all of my Adamic tendencies.

Joseph embraced a position of serving Mary, including the self-denial that it requires. He humbled himself and released the need to be seen as number one in his marriage. He did not protest that Mary got the first angelic encounter, that God didn't ask him before giving Mary such a significant calling, or that he wasn't called "highly favored" by the angel, as Mary was. Instead of feeling intimidated or threatened by Mary's significant call from God, he continued to serve her in humility.

Not only did he serve Mary, but he was also able to view her successes as his own because he loved Mary as he loved himself. For example, when she had a God encounter and received a special assignment from the angel, not only did Joseph not protest, but he treated it as a shared assignment. Instead of thinking in terms of *hers* and *mine*, he treated what she was carrying as *ours*. He even accepted and faithfully fathered a Child who was not his own. Because he owned his role as husband, Joseph was able to identify and embrace his call, which was wrapped up in serving Mary as she fulfilled the call on her life.

Joseph's selfless perspective prophetically declared what Paul spoke about in Ephesians, when he exhorted husbands to "love their wives as their own bodies. He who loves his wife loves himself. After all, no one ever hated their own body, but they feed and care for their body, just as Christ does the church" (5:28–29). This is the picture of marriage that God originally gave us in the garden, where the man laid down his life for his bride to emerge. Eve was from Adam's own body, and he would love her as his own body. They rose together in marital union, and they were united to each other.

The same call is extended to husbands today. You are called not only to be a husband to your wife but also to become a student of your wife so that you can know, love, and serve all of who she is, just as you would do for yourself. It's not something you can do from a place of disconnection from your wife. To live in this kind of love for and service of your wife, you need to spend focused time and energy to observe, listen to, study, and connect with your wife. You need to resist the simplistic desire to "fix" her or her struggles and, instead, listen with compassion. You need to invest in your connection and build a relationship that's a safe place for your wife's heart. Then, when you listen, there will be space for her to share her strengths and weaknesses, her gifts and callings, and her deeper hopes and dreams.

When Joseph began to understand the enormity of what God was doing on the inside of Mary, he dropped everything to support her and care for what God had placed inside of her. Husbands are called to the same radical response—to not only identify with but to spend themselves for the sake of their wives.

If you will emulate Joseph's example, I believe that the effects of Adam's model will begin to crumble before your eyes, and you will begin to experience God's original intent for marriage. Joseph's life is a pattern and preview of the restorative work that God was bringing to the earth through Jesus, who is God's Son and the Bridegroom to which God's story points.

Through Jesus, God not only restores humanity back to union with Himself, but He also removes the effects of the fall on man and woman, restoring them back to the unity and side-by-side relationship known before the fall. God chose Joseph, a just and righteous man, as a vessel who could handle this new-wineskin assignment without bursting, and you honor God by emulating his example as a godly husband who not only identified with his wife but spent his life to serve her.

BE AN INSTRUMENT

To conclude this section, I want to share one final aspect of what it means to be a Joseph by looking at the biblical account of another man named Joseph. The Book of Genesis chronicles the remarkable life of this Joseph, including his coat of many colors, being sold into slavery by his brothers, receiving dream interpretations from God, and becoming a powerful leader under Pharaoh in Egypt. I believe that the Genesis 30 account of Rachel giving birth to him shows us that God sends Josephs to be instruments of redemption, justice, and healing for women—His daughters, His precious ones whom He holds close to His heart.

The reason that Rachel conceived Joseph is because "God remembered Rachel; he listened to her and enabled her to conceive" (Gen. 30:22). If you read any of the previous verses in Genesis 30, it's clear that Rachel was in a difficult family situation. She suffered from infertility, and she was engulfed in a family conflict around her husband's other wife and two servants, who had conceived children with her husband, all while Rachel was still barren. But when God sent Joseph, Rachel proclaimed that God had removed her disgrace (v. 23), not unlike Mary's Joseph, who sought to protect her from "public disgrace" (Matt. 1:19). Through a vessel named Joseph, God removed disgrace from the women, mothers, daughters, and wives named Rachel and Mary. Josephs are an expression of God's heart of compassion for women.

I believe part of the identity of Josephs includes a call to be instruments of God-ordained redemption for women. It is a call to be men with hearts of justice and compassion for women near and far, partnering with God to bring healing, freedom, and restoration to women and championing God's call and purposes for their lives. It is a call to be an instrument used by God to bless and serve women, just as God used men named Joseph to bless and serve Rachel and Mary.

Just as with Adam and Eve in the beginning, God continued to tell His story through Mary and Joseph. God intentionally chose them to be Jesus' earthly parents, and with them He introduced a new breed of marriage covenant that echoes the heart of the Creator. For husbands seeking to step out of ungodly patterns and into God's plan for humankind, Joseph is a treasure and a model whose legacy leads us to the One to come after him.

REFLECTION QUESTIONS

- What are the main characteristics of Joseph's model as a husband?
- Do you identify with any of those characteristics? How so?
- What concepts in this chapter resonated with you the most?
- What are ways that you can serve your wife's call?

CHAPTER 4

Jesus:
The Love of a Husband

> As a bridegroom rejoices over his bride, so will
> your God rejoice over you.
> —Isaiah 62:5

I'm grateful that God did not leave me in Adam's fallen legacy. Jesus came and found me in my mess and in my darkness. Then He faithfully and gently led me into a life of purpose and identity with Him. I can't say it was a quick journey, but when you're with the One who is outside of time, the need to rush starts to fade.

Before Katie and I were married, years of my life resembled the brokenness of Adam's model. I was steeped in the insecurity, self-protection, secrecy, and separation that stem from the pride in Adam's example. I was struggling with addictions, broken and dysfunctional relationships, and a general sense of hopelessness.

After Katie and I were married, my emotional journey reminded me of when God delivered the Israelites from the Egyptians. It took a day to get out of Egypt, but it took years to recover from the oppression they experienced there. I, too, crossed the threshold into a new life in a day, but I still had a lot of emotional pain and dysfunction that I lived with on a regular basis. I was a difficult person to be around because of my own brokenness and insecurities.

As I walked forward with Katie and in my relationship with Jesus, I received a lot of healing and began to see change in my life. Where I used to shut down in conflict, I was able to share my emotions and stay present. Where I used to be inconsistent or hurtful to Katie, I learned how to express my needs and to be more relatable. It was a process, but even Katie affirms that I'm a different person than when we first got married.

I didn't really know how to manage myself in the first years of our marriage. I was in the trenches and trying not to hurt Katie. I wanted to be a good husband, but more than that, I was trying really hard not to be a bad one. When our first child, Ruby Joy, was born with a terminal disease, the pressure on our relationship only increased. As I reflect back on my immaturity and foolishness during that time, I believe that Jesus was laying the foundation for what I'm sharing in this book. In those times, I believe Jesus was beginning to invite me to take a higher way, to show me His view of marriage, and to show me how to be a godly husband who follows after His example.

I'm still learning and growing, and I'm not perfect. I'm still repenting, apologizing, healing, and maturing. So I'm not going to end this book by saying, "And that's how I became the perfect husband." But

I can say with confidence that Jesus makes all the difference. If you will come to Him, He will gladly meet you where you are and help you move forward.

Looking back at my step-by-step journey with Jesus over the years, I can see that He has done a work of transformation in my heart and life. I am no longer driven to my previous addictions, my wife attests that she hasn't experienced the older-sibling complex from me for years, and I'm in relationships that are the healthiest I've ever had. The cloud of hopelessness and depression I lived with for years has lifted, and I am experiencing real joy in my life. Underneath all of the issues in my life that God has addressed, I also know that He has been doing a deep work of healing in my heart, and the pains I accumulated over my life are being healed in the light of His kindness and strong love. I praise God for the way He's brought transformation in my life and in my marriage.

Marriage was created by God as a picture of His relationship with humankind, and it is important to His heart. Because of this, it would be wise for us to learn from Him about marriage and His intent for husbands. In the New Testament, Jesus, the last Adam, stepped onto the scene and gave us this living, breathing model of God's design for husbands.

JESUS, THE ONE TO COME

Adam was the original portrait of Christ, bearing His image and telling His story, but his life and legacy were marred by sin. The inaugural man's defining actions broke his union with God and shattered his marriage. As we behold Adam, the sound of that brokenness still reverberates down to us, a frequency resonant with our own souls. We are our father's sons, and he is the icon of those who have fallen short of their created purpose. Our countenances identify us with him and bear witness to our inherited estrangement.

Joseph and his wife, Mary, form the frame through which God literally birthed His redemptive plan for humankind. God chose to entrust His Word to a specific woman and a specific man. In a world full of husbands like Adam, Joseph was a husband who was boldly countercultural. Joseph was humble; Adam was prideful. Joseph feared God; Adam blamed Him. Joseph laid down his life for Mary; Adam sacrificed his connection with Eve. Joseph was a different kind of man—one whom God intentionally placed in this chapter of His story, heralding His redemption.

And now we come to Jesus, through whom we receive the gracious gift of rescue and restoration, God's "grand setting-everything-right" (Rom. 5:17, MSG). He is the Messiah, the Anointed One, the King of kings, and the Lord of lords.

Throughout the Bible, God's story with His people reflects God as a husband and His people as the bride. Isaiah told God's people that "your Maker is your husband—the LORD Almighty is his name" (Isa. 54:5). John the Baptist called Jesus the Bridegroom and gladly directed the bride of Christ to follow Jesus instead of himself (John 3:27–30). Jesus Himself used the bridegroom imagery during His earthly ministry (Matt. 25:1–13; Mark 2:19). Even in the final New Testament book, the Revelation of Jesus Christ, the marriage supper of the Lamb is part of its culmination (Rev. 19:6–9). Jesus is the Bridegroom.

Because of what Jesus did, men don't have to walk in Adam's footsteps of blame, isolation, and brokenness. Because of Jesus, we can see the way that is more excellent than the way Adam chose. Because of

Jesus, our model Bridegroom, we can better understand God's original intent for Adam, the first created husband. "Marriage is the beautiful design of the Almighty...meant to be a vivid example of Christ and his church" (Eph. 5:32, TPT). For husbands born into an Adamic world, the fact that Jesus is a husband and that He's modeled the way for us is very good news.

Paul exhorts husbands to love their wives as Christ loved the church, giving their lives up for their wives. Jesus the Bridegroom is an example for men as they relate to women, as well as for husbands as they relate to their wives. In His life, there are three main characteristics that make up His model for husbands. The first is the very essence of who God is.

AGAPE LOVE

Jesus passionately loves His bride, the church, and husbands are called to love their wives with this same love. At first glance, this looks like a basic truth placed unassumingly in the text of Ephesians 5:25. But taking a deeper look at the kind of love Jesus has for the church is important because the ancient Greek used in the New Testament is very different from present-day English, especially in its treatment of the concept of love.

The word *love* is used so broadly in the English language that it is easy to miss the deeper meaning of *love* in Ephesians 5:25. To the twenty-first century Christian in the English-speaking world, the word *love* is a common, everyday term used to mean many different things. A child loves his favorite stuffed animal. A husband loves his wife, and together they make love. A Christian woman loves God, but she may also love a good cup of coffee.

In ancient Greek, there was no single, all-encompassing word for *love* as there is in contemporary English. There were actually four different Greek words for *love*. Each of them has a unique meaning, but when translated, our English Bibles use the same word, *love*, for all four. To understand Jesus' love for His bride, it's important to differentiate between these four types of love found in the ancient Greek language. The four Greek words are *eros, phileo, storge,* and *agape*.

Eros love is that of sexual pleasure. It includes romantic or sexual love, and it is driven by attraction, desire, or lust for another. Its goal is sensual satisfaction. It's where the English word *erotic* comes from. Although romance and physical intimacy are important for Christian marriage, eros is not the love of Ephesians 5:25.

The next type of love is phileo love, which is brotherly love. It is an affection that is shared and mutual between two people, such as in the bond of friendship.[1] Every strong marriage needs this kind of committed and reciprocated love, but this is not the love of Ephesians 5:25 either.

Storge love is similar to phileo. It is a devoted love shown among family members. In Romans 12:10, it appears as *philostorgos*,[2] a compound of *phileo* and *storge*: "Love [*philostorgos*] one another with brotherly affection [*philadelphia*, from the root *phileo*]" (ESV). This verse describes love within the family of God, between brothers and sisters in Christ. Precious as it is, this also is not the love of Ephesians 5:25.

The love in Ephesians 5 is agape love. This is the love that Jesus has for His bride, and it is the same love that Paul calls husbands to have for their wives. Agape love is set apart from the other three. It is in a league of its own because *God is agape* love (1 John 4:8). It is the essence and character of God Himself, and so it is love supreme, the highest of all loves.

First John tells us, "This is how we know what [agape] love is: Jesus Christ laid down his life for us" (3:16). By looking to Jesus, we can see what this agape love looks like. Jesus is the perfect portrait of the agape love of God, for "God demonstrated his own [agape] love for us in this: While we were still sinners, Christ died for us" (Rom. 5:8). Jesus' life and example are inseparably linked to the expression of His agape love. And by following Him as our model, husbands can learn how to love their wives with this greatest love of all, the agape love of God commanded in Ephesians 5:25.

Jesus loved humankind before we ever had a thought of Him. He loved us while we were still stuck in our own messes. His love for us, His bride, exists independently from our performances, our failures, or even our successes because His love for us existed before we were even alive. No matter what we do, right or wrong, mature or immature, His love for us remains. We cannot earn it, and we cannot purchase it. He just loves us.

This agape love is altogether different than the love of the world we're born into as Adam's sons. That's the reason one of Jesus' first words when He started His earthly ministry was "Repent"—He thinks differently than we do (Matt. 4:17). The erotic love of eros seeks self-gratification; agape love is for the sake of the other. Phileo and storge expect mutual benefit; agape love is an unwavering force with or without reciprocation. This love sows and sows and sows, regardless of what it reaps. This is the selfless, unchanging, face-like-flint love of God; He loves us because He loves us because He loves us because He loves us.

Jesus' burning passion for His bride is like a steady one-way arrow pointed in her direction. He burns with a consuming love that will not be quenched. His posture of love for her is fixed, and nothing His bride can do will change that. It cannot be shut down, controlled, or stifled by anyone—ever. Jesus' love for His bride is constant. He loves her because He loves her because He loves her because He loves her.

Husbands are to posture their hearts in that same unconditional, unrelenting, everlasting love for their wives. There is no justifiable reason to withhold or diminish this posture of love, for it is fueled and sustained by God Himself. This love is a reflection of the perfect agape love of God for humanity, and its white-hot flame should burn regardless of your wife's performance, reciprocation, or anything else.

Jesus loves His bride with the greatest love of all, the agape love of God. This love is the motivation and foundation of the 5:25 call.

SELF-SACRIFICE

Agape love is not only the essence of God's character, but its selfless, passionate nature must find expression through action. Just as God demonstrated His own love for us by dying for us, so must our agape love be demonstrated by its expression (Rom. 5:8).

The word *expression* comes from two words: *ex*, which means out, and *press*, like a French press that forces hot water over coffee beans to make coffee. Putting these two concepts together, when you express yourself, you are pressing your heart from an internal reality into an external demonstration so that it finds expression outside of yourself. You are allowing the contents of your heart to be made manifest through expression so you can share your heart with others.

The interesting thing is that without even trying, you're always expressing something of your internal reality. It's an automatic and unavoidable aspect of being a human. Proverbs puts it this way: "Above all, guard the affections of your heart, for they affect all that you are.

Pay attention to the welfare of your innermost being, for from there flows the wellspring of life" (4:23, TPT).

The question is not whether you will share your internal reality with the world around you. The question is, what do your words and actions prove is in your heart? When you get squeezed, does agape love come out, or does something else get expressed? The fruit of my life testifies of what is in my heart. If I have agape love in my heart for my wife, then my life will attest to that fact. If my words and actions look more like Adam's model, then my lack of agape love will be self-evident.

Jesus' heart is full of agape love for His bride, and one of the primary ways He expressed and demonstrated this love was through His self-sacrifice for her sake. In Ephesians 5 terms, husbands are to express agape love for their wives just as Christ loved the church and gave Himself up for her.

The Greek word for *gave* in Ephesians 5:25—"Christ…gave himself up for her"—is *paradidōmi*. It means to hand over, deliver, or betray. It means to give oneself up, even to death, for another.[3] Jesus betrayed Himself and gave up His own self-interest for the sake of the church. His example was in direct opposition to Adam, who willingly sacrificed his connection with Eve for self-protection. Agape love and self-sacrifice are very different from Adam's model, and by understanding Jesus' thoughts, we will see just how extreme those differences are.

THINKING LIKE JESUS

In Philippians, Paul shared precious insights into Jesus' loving act of sacrifice for the church. Paul taught the Philippians about the inner thoughts, or mind, of Christ and encouraged them to have the same perspective:

> Let each of you look not to your own interests, but to the interests of others. Let the same mind be in you that was in Christ Jesus, who, though he was in the form of God, did not regard equality with God as something to be exploited, but emptied himself, taking the form of a slave, being born in human likeness. And being found in human form, he humbled himself and became obedient to the point of death—even death on a cross.
>
> —PHILIPPIANS 2:4–8, NRSV

In these verses, Paul revealed how Jesus viewed His self-emptying sacrifice of love, and it is instructive for husbands called to be like Him. The pivotal verse in this passage is verse 7, which says He "emptied himself." This parallels the Ephesians 5 description of Christ giving up His life for His bride. The Greek word used in this verse for *emptied* is *kenoō*, and it is connected to Jesus' sacrifice on the cross. It means to make empty, to neutralize, or to make of no reputation.[4] Other translations describe Jesus' act of self-emptying similarly, saying that He:

- "made himself nothing by taking the very nature of a servant" (Phil. 2:7)
- "gave up his divine privileges" (NLT)
- "made himself of no reputation" (KJV)

For husbands, this is where the rubber meets the road. You must choose to express agape love to your wife, even when it's inconvenient and even when there are other options pulling at you. Your agape love must find expression in your actions, even when it's costly.

This is in stark contrast to Adam's model. Instead of choosing to give himself away, Adam withheld and separated himself from Eve and God. His model teaches us to seek after power selfishly, not to give it away. It teaches us to preserve our reputations and self-protect.

There are many temptations available for husbands seeking to avoid self-sacrifice. Some of these may even appear to be noble or holy, but the fruit of these decisions reveals their true motive. For example, it's tempting for a man in Adam's model to justify self-serving activities by claiming they are for the benefit of his wife or family. Working long hours and through the weekends can be justified as providing a certain standard of living, or the husband can even deflect the real issue by accusing his wife of being ungrateful. But did she ask for that "perk" that requires her to trade her connection with her husband for things money can buy?

For some men, deep down in the caverns of their souls, they have hearts that are afraid of relationship, that avoid vulnerability, and that are terrified of being known. Seeking an out, you may embrace busyness, workaholism, and the tyranny of self-importance to drown out the voices of fear, but these things also drown out the needs, cries, and pleas of those closest to you. Justifying yourself by your activity, you refuse to give up your life and stubbornly persist in hiding from the truth. But the husband who would rather do things for his wife than be connected to her is protecting his prideful independence, and underneath it all, he's refusing to die to himself.

A similar delusion that seeks to seduce men is the belief that being willing to die for someone is the same as actually dying for that person, but the two are very different. Your faith must be demonstrated through your actions; your love must find expression. In Ephesians, Paul didn't say, "Husbands, be willing to love your wives like Christ did." He said emphatically, "Love your wives, just as Christ...gave himself up" (Eph. 5:25). Claiming that you're willing to die for your spouse is like telling the IRS that you're willing to pay your taxes—it may feel adequate, but it falls short of what's actually required, and you'll suffer for it. You have to act on that willingness.

The following example from Jesus' ministry demonstrates the difference between being willing and following through:

> A man with leprosy came to him and begged him on his knees, "If you are willing, you can make me clean."
>
> Jesus was indignant. He reached out his hand and touched the man. "I am willing," he said. "Be clean!" Immediately the leprosy left him and he was cleansed."
>
> —Mark 1:40-42

Jesus is not satisfied for us to know that He can heal us; He heals us! And men walking in Jesus' model cannot be satisfied with giving lip service to this directive. This deception is a trap of the enemy that tries to sooth your conscience with the illusion of obedience to God, when in reality you are staring at your cross instead of carrying it. Not only are you disobedient, but you think you are obeying! But Jesus' call requires both heart and action: "Whoever wants to be my disciple must deny themselves and take up their cross daily and follow me. For whoever wants to save their life will lose it, but whoever loses their life for me will save it" (Luke 9:23–24).

The supposed willingness to die does not actually require love or sacrifice. It is worlds apart from a man who makes the daily choice of denying himself, taking up his cross, and following Jesus. This is the man who prefers his wife, lives out agape love, and pours his life out for her. Charles Spurgeon is often credited with saying that he could find ten men willing to die for the Bible for every one who was willing to read it. I wonder: of every ten husbands who are willing to die for their wives, how many would love their wives through sacrificial changes such as changing a job, hobby, or lifestyle to directly benefit their wives or build a stronger connection with them? Jesus did not remain in heaven, knowing He was willing to die for the world. He took decisive action at extreme personal expense to pour Himself out in agape love for us. His love was expressed through action.

Sometimes I wonder if the struggle to walk as an Ephesians 5:25 man has something to do with the conceptual nature of the giving up of oneself. It's easy to know when I've sent an email, changed the oil in my car, or eaten lunch, but honestly, trying to think of a practical way to give up myself for my wife can feel very abstract. It's difficult to check the box that says I've successfully given myself up for my wife today, because it's not always easy to quantify. It takes some effort, thought, and processing to find life application for this verse in the twenty-first century, but here are some examples of what Jesus' self-sacrifice looked like:

- Jesus didn't defend Himself or strive to preserve His place. Even when facing His accusers, He had the self-control, security, and fortitude to remain silent (Isa. 53:7).
- Jesus surrendered His rights and privileges; He relinquished His exalted place (Phil. 2:6).
- He put His reputation through the shredder (Phil. 2:7).

- He made Himself nothing (Phil. 2:7).
- He became a servant (Phil. 2:7).
- He humbled Himself to obey God with His whole heart (Phil. 2:8).
- He obeyed God, even when it killed Him (Phil. 2:8).

Jesus was not satisfied to *appear* as loving or sacrificial. He *was* loving. He *was* sacrificial. He showed us what agape love looks like, and He has called us to follow in His footsteps.

FALSE HUMILITY

Before I move on to the next attribute of Jesus' model, I want to mention a specific enemy of those seeking to follow Jesus: false humility. For Christian men who are already spending themselves in service to others, giving of yourself may be a natural thing for you to do. But if that's the case for you, then you may struggle with allowing Jesus to grow you into more than a servant. Serving others is an integral part of following Jesus that you don't outgrow, but if you stop at serving others, then you are in danger of disobeying Jesus when He says to you, "Friend, move up to a better place" (Luke 14:10). If you fall into false humility, you are in danger of staying in the grave when He shows up to resurrect you in power. Don't let false humility keep you from what Jesus purchased for you. False humility seeks to convince you to forfeit your inheritance in God and to feel proud of it. In reality, that's not humility at all.

For the man who has been derailed by false humility, his sacrifice can actually be fueled by self-protection and an aversion to vulnerability and connection—the very things that agape love sacrifices for. Even in marriage, a husband can use positive behaviors, such as serving and championing his wife's purpose or calling, to make sure that no one ever opens up the grave he's dug for himself in the name of sacrificial love. Fear of failure, fear of rejection, and other negative views of self can drive these seemingly positive behaviors, but they are rooted in the pride of false humility.

Self-sacrifice must be fueled by agape love, and the goal of that love is the connection, relationship, and intimacy found in union.

UNION

Jesus recalled God's original design for marriage, stating, "From the beginning God created male and female. For this reason a man will leave his parents and be wedded to his wife. And the husband and wife will be joined as one flesh, and after that they no longer exist as two, but one flesh. So there you have it. What God has joined together, no one has the right to split apart" (Mark 10:6–9, TPT). These themes of intimacy and union are proclaimed throughout God's story, and they are the goal of His love and sacrifice for His bride.

As Jesus approached the final hours before His crucifixion, He told us what consumed His thoughts and feelings. Nearing His supreme act of self-emptying love, Jesus was consumed with relationship. To His disciples He spoke, "Greater [agape] love has no one than this: to lay down one's life for one's friends....I no longer call you servants.... Instead, I have called you friends" (John 15:13, 15). No longer would Jesus tolerate only a master-servant relationship with His bride. He was announcing a drastic change in this relationship, and it was being accomplished by His own sacrifice. I imagine the disciples staring blankly, unable to take in the enormity of His invitation. The covenant invitation from the Last Supper was extended to them in friendship, connection, and union, not in terms of the fall and His ruling over them.

God was making a way for people to reenter the place of sweet fellowship with the Creator that was lost in the fall. They would have restored fellowship with God and walk with Him in the garden of delight—in friendship and, yes, even in marriage.

The voice of the Bridegroom rose again in John 17. Continuing His theme from the Last Supper, Jesus' thoughts and prayers in the Garden of Gethsemane were about being united with His bride: "Father, I want those you have given me to be with me where I am" (v. 24). Jesus earnestly desired union with His bride, and He paid a great personal sacrifice to get her back.

Ever since God separated the first human into male and female, there has been an acute awareness of our need for intimacy and connection. Since the beginning, we have had needs that can't be met without connection, but because we have the freedom to choose, connection is vulnerable. It's risky, and it comes with a cost. Vulnerability and honesty, truth and nakedness, trust and commitment, covenant and sacrifice—they are all expensive. They are all risky. Opening your heart to love also opens it to pain. But closing your heart to pain also closes it to love. There's a lot to lose and a lot to gain when you choose to venture out from isolation and to wade into the waters of connection with others.

To Jesus, the benefits of union far outweighed the costs. He had lost His intimate connection with humanity in the fall, but He was determined to have it back. As He said in John 17, Jesus' desire was to have His bride with Him, and He would do what it took to restore that connection and union.

I believe Jesus' heart cry from John 17—to get back what was lost in the garden—permeated His ministry. Just looking at some of the parables that Jesus gave, His burning desire to get back what was lost echoed through His teachings:

- The parable of the lost sheep describes the shepherd who leaves ninety-nine sheep to pursue one. When he has rescued it, he proclaims, "Rejoice with me; I have found my lost sheep" (Luke 15:3–7).
- The parable of the lost coin describes a woman who turns her whole house upside down to find a lost coin. When she has found it, she proclaims, "Rejoice with me; I have found my lost coin" (Luke 15:8–10).
- The parable of the lost son describes a father's son who runs away. But when the son returns home, the father proclaims, "Let's have a feast and celebrate. For this son of mine was dead and is alive again; he was lost and is found" (Luke 15:11–32).
- The parable of the hidden treasure is about a man who found hidden treasure and "in his joy went and sold all he had and bought that field" (Matt.13:44).
- The parable of the pearl is about a merchant searching for fine pearls, and "when he found one of great value, he went away and sold everything he had and bought it" (Matt. 13:45–46).

In each of these passages, something of extreme value was lost or missing, and the main character did whatever it took to obtain the lost treasure. Each time, the main character paid a price, even selling everything, to obtain that which brought him or her so much joy.

Jesus was not intimidated by the cost of union. The very thought of being united to His bride brought Him great joy and made the cost more than worth it. His heart was set on a goal "like a champion rejoicing to run his course" (Ps. 19:5). With the true heart of a Bridegroom, Jesus resolutely pursued His goal of removing the chasm between God and humanity.

The Servant of all gave a great sacrifice so that He would have togetherness with His bride from then on. He restored the original intent of union—first of God with humanity and then of man and woman in marriage.

It is with this determination and with this knowing that Jesus willingly sacrificed His life. At the Last Supper, Jesus revealed the reality those parables spoke of. Each of the parables expressed the cry of His heart, which was about to give the greatest demonstration of agape love, and He wanted them to know that He did it with them in mind. "Greater [agape] love has no one than this: to lay down one's life for one's friends....I no longer call you servants....Instead, I have called you friends" (John 15:13, 15).

For the Bridegroom, the bride is the hidden treasure that He is overjoyed to have back. She is the lost coin that He's turned His world upside down to gain. He rejoices over her and His eyes of fire burn for her. She is His pearl, and their union is full of fiery agape love.

> My passion is stronger than the chains of death and the grave, all consuming as the very flashes of fire from the burning heart of God. Place this fierce, unrelenting fire over your entire being. Rivers of pain and persecution will never extinguish this flame. Endless floods will be unable to quench this raging fire that burns

within you. Everything will be consumed. It will stop at nothing as you yield everything to this furious fire until it won't even seem to you like a sacrifice anymore.

—SONG OF SONGS 8:6–7, TPT

His sacrifice on the cross was a violent act against anything that hinders our love relationship with Him, for He desires proximity, intimacy, and union with His bride. Because of Jesus, the bride can say with confidence, "Absolutely *nothing* can get between us and God's love" (Rom. 8:39, MSG). Jesus' great sacrifice on the cross purchased union and restored relationship with His bride. This is the Bridegroom's desire, and it is both the motivation of His sacrifice and the goal of His agape love.

UNION WITH CHRIST

For those who accept Jesus' invitation through His body and blood, a whole new life begins. However, just like Adam and Eve stepped out of God's best for their relationship, it is possible for God's blood-bought people to also live at a distance from their Bridegroom, not knowing that their lives with God are hidden with Christ (Col. 3:3).

Paul's writings in the New Testament give us insight into the New Covenant union between God and His people, and its implications for the marriage union between a man and a woman.

Union is the result of being united with Christ. Through His death and resurrection, we have been reconciled to God, and now no one can separate us from His love (Rom. 8:38–39). Throughout the New Testament, and especially in Paul's writings, we learn about this new life in Christ and what it means to be united with Him. The New

Testament defines this dynamic life, and through it we learn that union is a foundational and integral theme to the New Covenant proposal Christ extended to us.

The level of connection, togetherness, and intimacy given to us in Christ is striking. Below is a short list of New Testament verses that describe the relationship between Jesus and the church:

- The bride of Christ has been crucified with Christ and buried with Him (Gal. 2:20; Col. 2:12), and we are baptized into Him and His death (Rom. 6:3).
- The bride of Christ is raised with Christ and united with Him in His resurrection (Rom. 6:5).
- The bride of Christ is seated with Him in heavenly places (Eph. 2:6).
- The bride of Christ is an heir with Christ (Rom. 8:17).
- The bride of Christ will rule with Christ (2 Tim. 2:12; Rev. 3:21).
- The bride of Christ is in Christ, and He is in us (1 Cor. 1:30; 2 Cor. 13:5); the church is one flesh with Christ (Eph. 5:31–32).
- The body of Christ is called to attain the whole measure of the fullness of Christ (Eph. 4:13).

Through these verses, it's obvious that not only is Jesus passionate about being connected to His bride, but He also wants to do life with her and have that connection and union permeate His life. He desires for her to be with Him where He is (John 17:24).

Finding application for these concepts in marriage, however, is not always easy. In an effort to make them more practical for marriage, I've created the following list of truths for husbands based on Jesus' example. I encourage you to read through them, connect with these aspects of Jesus' heart, and adopt them into your own heart posture toward your wife. Biblical references below can be found in the previous list.

1. As a husband, I cultivate agape love that is a constant stream of devotion, affection, and commitment to my wife.

My love is loyal and stays "on," regardless of the actions, words, performance, or reciprocation of my wife. My love refuses to publicly expose my wife's weakness or mistakes but instead gives of itself to honor and protect her.

2. Marriage is a call for me to die to myself and my privileges and for me to step into new life in union with my wife.

There is no area of my life that can enter into the marriage covenant without passing through the cross. Saying yes to my wife is an unequivocal no to all others. I do not entertain things that hinder our love relationship. Past identities, privileges, and entitlements that will not come under the umbrella of this union are left in the grave, but we are raised together into a shared life of resurrection power.

3. The goal of the marriage relationship is to establish and grow connection and intimacy.

We are in Him, and He is in us. Dividing walls in my marriage relationship can be healed as I set my heart to daily strengthen and deepen our connection. I shed ungodly independence and embrace the "usness" of the two becoming one in a God-centered marriage. What was mine before the wedding is ours in marriage. I don't lose my identity as an individual, but I grow into a relationship of interdependence.

In this relationship, I identify with her, I share myself honestly, I listen to and learn about her, and I continue pursuing deeper connection.

4. There's room for both the husband and wife to be powerful.

The bride is seated with Christ in heavenly places, and He has given her authority. I refuse to pick up Adam's fallen model that shuns co-leadership and only allows the husband to be powerful. I insist on both the husband and wife being empowered in the marriage and bringing their unique expressions of the image of God. The diversity of our strengths, weaknesses, experience, and perspectives is an asset, not a liability. We are on the same team, we are fully committed, and we use our power to serve one another in love.

5. Resurrection power and Holy Spirit empowerment are the inheritance of those who embrace the cross.

Habitual sin, ungodly generational patterns, and excuses of powerlessness end with me. I am given power to live the model of Jesus as I am transformed into the likeness of Christ. By the power of the Spirit and the blood of Jesus, I throw off familiar sins along with the temptation to blame God, my wife, or my life circumstances. I take personal responsibility for my life, and I press on to take hold of that for which Christ Jesus so radically took hold of me.

LIGHT IN THE DARKNESS

As I meditate on these five truths about Jesus' model as husband, different emotions surface within me. I feel grateful that Jesus came and showed us a better way. I also feel convicted that the effects of

Adam's model are far worse than I had realized. I feel hope for myself and countless others because of Jesus. Because of Him, transformation is possible. As I finish this chapter, I find myself marveling at who Jesus is and the high value He places on connection and union with His bride. Reflecting on Him as a Bridegroom, a sense of awe comes over me and the words of Job come to mind: "My ears had heard of you but now my eyes have seen" (Job 42:5).

Adam's sons only saw covenant that was marred by brokenness. They lived in the perpetual reverberations of the fall and all the subsequent destruction. Their separation from the Light of the world darkened every area of their lives, including their covenant relationships. But thanks be to God, Jesus the Bridegroom invaded this darkness with His love's pure light. Adam's sons can now see the light shining, of which Adam was only a silhouette (Rom. 5:14). And in the Book of Revelation, the last Adam extended an invitation to us that the first could not; He said to us, "To the one who is victorious, I will give the right to eat from the tree of life" (Rev. 2:7). Through Jesus' love and sacrifice, He has made a way for us to step back into the paradise of His presence and to eat from the tree of life. In the same way, He has opened the door for husbands and wives to experience His original intent for the marriage union in the garden of delight.

By living in union with Jesus, we learn how He relates to the bride of Christ. And in that personal revelation of the Bridegroom and His bride, husbands are equipped to turn and love their wives just as Christ loved the church, by giving Himself up for her.

REFLECTION QUESTIONS

- What are the main characteristics of Jesus' model as a husband?
- Do you identify with any of those characteristics? How so?
- What concepts in this chapter resonated with you the most?
- What is Jesus' heart for His bride? How does that impact your aspirations as a husband?

CHAPTER 5

The Call

> Husbands, love your wives, just as Christ loved the church and gave himself up for her to make her holy, cleansing her by the washing with water through the word, and to present her to himself as a radiant church, without stain or wrinkle or any other blemish, but holy and blameless.
> —Ephesians 5:25–27

It was a normal work day for me, just like any other. But as the day progressed, it became one that I'll never forget. As I went through my work day, a strange sensation came over me. I had an unusual awareness of the side of my body like I'd never felt before. The sensation started lightly, but it persisted and increased throughout the day.

THE CREDENTIAL

I wasn't sure what was happening, but my left ribs felt as if something were pressing against them from the outside. Trying to understand, I ran my hands over my ribs. Was it an injury or a bruise? Maybe I ran into something over the last few days, and my body was reminding me. But I found nothing on my body to explain it. The sensation continued in a place on my rib cage just a few inches wide. What was it? I didn't feel any cuts, bruises, or other indicators. I had no idea what the feeling was.

I continued throughout my day with this sensation pressing against me. As I thought and prayed, it occurred to me that maybe it wasn't physical. Maybe it was spiritual. If God was speaking to me through this sensation, I wondered what it would mean. With a new set of lenses, I sought His voice and began to process my experience on a spiritual level. I considered what God might be saying about my rib cage on the left side of my body.

It occurred to me that ribs are mentioned in the Bible. In Genesis, God pulled materials out of Adam's side that He used to create Eve. Translations often refer to this material as Adam's rib. The Bible also talks about Jesus' side. When He hung on the cross, "one of the soldiers pierced Jesus' side with a spear, bringing a sudden flow of blood and water" (John 19:34). This piercing was part of the Creator's plan, for not only did it resemble Adam's prophetic narrative in the creation account, but we know from the Book of John that it was also a fulfillment of Zechariah's words from the Old Testament, "They will look on the one they have pierced" (John 19:37; see also Zech. 12:10). This was Jesus, the One who was "pierced for our transgressions" (Isa. 53:5).

Meditating further, I considered the connection of Adam's side to Eve and of Jesus' side to the church. Adam's bride was brought from his side after he laid down his life; so too was Jesus' side pierced for His bride and His body was laid in the grave. My thoughts accelerated, and I began to connect the dots: God is calling men to lay down their lives for their wives so they can then rise together in resurrection life. As I pondered this pattern, different moments from the last few years came to mind.

Death was no stranger to Katie and me. During the first years of our marriage, we went through unthinkable tragedy, loss, and grief. Our daughter Ruby Joy was born with a terminal disease, and she suffered terribly for almost three years before she passed away.

When Ruby was with us, we were in a constant storm of pain, suffering, and medical care that crowded out normal family life. Katie and I were thrust into a chaotic world of hospitals, caregiving, and suffering. When Ruby passed away, Katie and I were left with the hollow echo of her life and an overwhelming sense of emptiness.

When Ruby was with us, Katie took on primary care for her while I worked full-time. I felt a little like Joseph, doing what he could to take care of Mary while she did the hard work of carrying, delivering, and nurturing the new life she had been given. My days were full of mundane meetings and spreadsheets, and my nights were swept away by the overwhelming world of medical care, suffering, and trying to have a fatherly relationship with my daughter while she suffered under the weight of disease. Our sleep was constantly interrupted by tube-feeding alarms, Ruby getting sick in the night, or the slightest noise triggering the panic that we had slept while Ruby needed us.

Our days and nights were full of trauma and pain until the assault of disease ended, but it took Ruby. Our world crumbled, and we collapsed in the crater of loss. As we sat in the shock and pain of loss, the world moved on. We tried to make sense of it all. Katie couldn't sustain a job due to her emotional pain. She was trying to reconcile her now-empty world with her previous life with Ruby, in which she had been so heartily invested. I continued working my job as a government contractor, but I was dying further as I sat at work and stared blankly at my screen between the ninety-minute commutes. We struggled hard to keep our heads above the quicksand of grief.

After two years of grieving and processing loss, we felt the release to move from the DC area and get a fresh start. On Easter of that year, we stumbled upon a small town outside of Lancaster, Pennsylvania, called Mount Joy. It was our escape from our grief-stricken lives in Virginia, and its name held a connection with Ruby Joy that gave us comfort in a time when few things could. The comfort we felt at the thought of moving to Mount Joy was itself a confirmation. We hadn't felt joy or hope like that in a long time. We took the leap and moved to Amish country in central Pennsylvania, a land filled with green fields and big, blue skies.

In time, Katie started a new endeavor and began attending ministry school. It was a sign of healing and personal breakthrough, even if our souls were still frail. I pledged my support, and I continued my long commute to work while she gained fortitude in our new life.

In that time of my life, I felt purposeless. I thought I was a dad, but I didn't have my daughter with me. I knew I was a husband, but our marriage was in survival mode as we tried to put the pieces together from our own ground zero. Our relationship was in its own orbit, pulled off center by grief's gravity. My routine was to drive, work, drive, and sleep. I was supporting Katie to have a new chapter, something she desperately needed. But my support for her didn't feel like nobility; it felt like survival. When I sacrificed for her, I wasn't swept into grandiose visions of the angels in heaven applauding my sacrifice. My highest hope for that time was that somehow, somewhere, in the midst of the mystery, pain, and loss, we would not quit.

Coming back to the sensation on my side, Adam's rib and Jesus' side felt significant to me. God was speaking about the role of husbands in relation to their wives. As I pondered what this could mean for me personally, a revelation suddenly surged within me: *"This is your credential, and it is recognized in heaven."* The imagery struck me. I know about credentials; I've spent a lot of time in pursuit of them. But I never imagined God would speak about them as a spiritual reality. Never had I received a credential like this. Paul's words to the Corinthians came to my mind:

> Does it sound like we're patting ourselves on the back, insisting on our credentials, asserting our authority? Well, we're not. Neither do we need letters of endorsement, either to you or from you. You yourselves are all the endorsement we need. Your very lives are a letter that anyone can read by just looking at you. Christ himself wrote it—not with ink, but with God's living Spirit; not chiseled into stone, but carved into human lives—and we publish it.
>
> —2 Corinthians 3:1–3, MSG

Marveling at the revelation unfolding before me, I felt God speaking through the picture of a wounded side to affirm that I was finishing strong in a race He had called me to. I was finishing a spiritual degree program of sorts, modeled after His intended design for Adam. And found in Jesus is the Author's redemption, where the blood and water flowed from the incision in His side as proof that He went the distance and laid down His life for His bride.

This revelation had my mind spinning. Could this really be God? Does God care this much about how I relate to Katie? Had God seen me as I served and sacrificed for my wife? Was it important enough to Him that He was recognizing it?

My questions turned to tears as I finally let His compassion in. I was being validated and affirmed in my role as a husband—and God was the One bringing it up! My heart was healing as He called my name. Times in my life I viewed as fruitless toil were flooding my mind as He honored me, gave me a fresh impartation, and invited me into resurrection life. Just as Jesus wasn't left in the grave, I felt that God was coming to find me in my grave and taking me from death to resurrection life. I had embraced sacrificial love for my bride, even in circumstances I did not want, and now He was inviting me into resurrection life alongside my wife—a place I could have reached only by following Jesus and submitting to the death and burial of my fallen life, passing through the cross and into new life in Him. And yet, as part of His bride, even this was a gift of grace to me.

THE 5:25 CALL

Under the banner of Ephesians 5:25, this book has explored the love relationship of God and humanity, of husband and wife. In this profound verse, Paul gave us a glimpse into the mystery that is the connection between Christ and the church and between husbands and wives.

Ephesians 5:25 is found in Paul's letter to the church in Ephesus, and it falls within the context of a larger conversation. Before Paul's instructions to husbands, he opened his discourse on relationships by giving these instructions: "Submit to one another out of reverence for Christ" (Eph. 5:21).

Next, he applied that relational dynamic to husbands and wives: "Wives, submit yourselves to your own husbands as you do to the Lord" (Eph. 5:22). It is important to note that the Greek word for *submit* in verse 22 is not found in the earliest manuscripts of this verse. Instead of writing the word for *submit* again in this verse, Paul instead referred to his previous command to submit to one another in verse 21: "Submit to one another out of reverence for Christ." This means that discussing "Wives, submit to your husbands" without the context of "Submit to one another" yields only a partial truth. If a husband recites the "submit" of verse 22 to his wife while neglecting the "one another" of the previous verse, he resembles Adam's model rather than Jesus' model. Zeroing in on verse 22 avoids the husband's personal responsibility from verses 21 and 25, and instead hypocritically points a finger at the one he loves. A man who is fixated on his wife's submission may have a plank in his eye—one that should be used to build the cross he's carrying to the end of himself.

Coming to the husband's responsibility in Ephesians 5:25, Paul gives the exhortation, "Husbands, love your wives, just as Christ loved the church and gave himself up for her." The passage continues by giving additional information about Christ's sacrifice, "to make her holy, cleansing her by the washing with water through the word, to present her to himself as a radiant church, without stain or wrinkle or any other blemish, but holy and blameless" (vv. 26–27).

As I read through this verse and considered Jesus' example, I saw that the purpose of Jesus giving up Himself was "to present her to himself." And in those few words, the model of Jesus and the 5:25 call are explained. "Christ…gave himself up for her…to present her to himself" (vv. 25, 27). Jesus' agape love drove Him to sacrifice in order to be connected and united with His bride. This is the heart of the Bridegroom, and this is the context for the 5:25 call.

Brothers, husbands, and men, I am calling you to respond to the 5:25 call. I believe this call did not originate with me but in the heart of God. Whether you are single, married, or divorced, whether you are young or old, I am inviting you to join me in following Jesus' model in our marriages and then exporting His love to the world by laying down our rights, fighting for women, and leaving a legacy.

LAY DOWN YOUR RIGHTS

In the progression of Adam, Joseph, and Jesus, God gave us a map to chart our way back to Him and His intended design for humanity. Any map is helpful for navigation only once you have a "you are here" marker to know where you are starting from.

Though Jesus came and showed us His original intent for husbands and wives, much of the world is still following Adam's example, which teaches men to protect their own rights and neglect the well-being of others. And Adam's model is not only being practiced, but it is also being taken to new extremes of brokenness on a global scale.

One consequence of the fall was that Adam would rule over Eve. What started in seed form with Adam's model has grown to epic proportions and enveloped civilizations, cultures, and people groups all over the world. In these environments, men have been elevated above women, and women have been made subject to men. This dismisses the original commission that Adam and Eve received, and it omits Jesus' sacrifice on the cross that removes the effects of the fall. Sometimes these dynamics are obvious through laws, customs, or policies, and other times they are invisible to the naked eye, planted deep within the thoughts of our subconscious minds.

SCHEMES AGAINST MEN

I believe one reason Adam's model is so familiar is because it is not purely Adam's. The profile of a fallen husband bears the fingerprints of the enemy. It is energized and perpetuated by Satan, for it is a continuation of his schemes against God and humanity in Genesis 3. In the garden, the serpent left Adam alone and did not speak directly to him. In the same way, the schemes of the enemy against men may not always look or feel evil. Sometimes the goal of the enemy is for men to be ignorant, absent, or even passive—as was seen with Adam. The enemy will also work to incentivize men to be passive, just as Adam's actions of self-protection worked for his self-interest. When God gave Adam and Eve over to their choices, they inherited him ruling over her. It was a dynamic that the enemy would use against men and women for centuries to come.

One way that Adam's model manifests in contemporary culture is through something called male privilege. Male privilege consists of the rights, advantages, or benefits given to men that are not given to women on the basis of their gender. It exists when men, knowingly or unknowingly, refuse to follow Jesus' model of agape love, sacrificial love, and connection with others. In following Adam's model, it is tempting to justify separation from those who are different from us. Just as Adam pointed the finger at Eve while refusing to take personal responsibility, male privilege accepts benefits at the expense of women. In essence, it seeks to perpetuate relational dynamics from the fall, and it refuses Jesus' restoration, purchased at the cross.

As with other injustices, it's easy to dismiss the reality of male privilege if you aren't personally impacted by it in a negative way. It's very easy to passively ignore, reactively discount, or seek to discredit claims that could reflect badly on a demographic you're a part of, whether it's your gender, race, etc. When taking this position, it's easy to believe the worst about "them" and the best about "us." Naturally, we identify with things true to our experiences, and we don't fully understand things outside of our experiences. But if I fall within a category that is privileged, such as being a male, I can be confident that it will be hard for me to accurately see the negative impact it has on others from my lone vantage point. For people who have privileges in this way, awareness of the existence of privilege is the first need. I'll share some global statistics about this dynamic in this chapter, but first, let's consider some lessons from the garden.

THE CAMPAIGN AGAINST WOMEN

The incentives that Satan offers to men through male privilege may have some perceived benefits, but there is a hidden agenda behind it. The many rights and advantages that men enjoy through male privilege come at a great cost to women today. And this also carries the enemy's fingerprints, for, in Genesis 3 God clearly declared to the serpent, "I will put enmity between you and the woman" (v. 15). The word used for *enmity* in this verse can mean hatred and hostility,[1] and this is what God placed between the enemy and Eve.

The enemy's hatred and hostility from Genesis is still aimed at Eve's daughters today, and the effects are seen on a global scale. Based on research from the Salvation Army's International Social Justice Commission, I've given a few examples below that start to illustrate the impact of this satanic hatred of our sisters and the enemy's campaign against them:

> Women often experience systemic social injustice because of their gender. Sexism can result in extreme human cruelty and even death....
>
> - Women have been doused in kerosene and set ablaze or burned with acid for 'disobedience.' So-called 'honour killings' take the lives of thousands of young women every year.
> - Globally, women aged 15 through 44 are more likely to be maimed or die from male violence than from cancer, malaria, traffic accidents and war combined.
> - The majority of people trapped in modern slavery every year are female, many being exploited for sexual purposes.
>
> Sexist attitudes may result in a pay gap or sexual harassment.... The feminisation of poverty is a direct consequence of women's unequal access to education and economic opportunities.

> The United Nations estimates that women perform 66 percent of the world's work and produce 50 percent of the food, yet earn only 10 percent of the income and own 1 percent of the property.[2]

> While both men and women are pornographic subjects, pornography frequently denigrates and objectifies women in particular, and as a result devalues their humanity and equality with men.[3]

The global dynamics represented have no resemblance to the garden paradise that Adam and Eve were created for. They do, however, have a striking resemblance to Adam's model and Satan's hatred of women. These high-level statistics are red flags indicating that the enemy is raging against our sisters, daughters, and mothers with terrible and far-reaching impact on women.

In the enemy's two-phased attack against women, he also seeks to disarm men and lull them to sleep with the perceived benefits of the fall while he wages war against women. Male privilege is a sleeping pill that uses comforts to insulate men from the plight of the women around them. Many times, if someone tries to wake them from their slumber into reality, they just grumble and go back to sleep.

For some of us, the effects of Adam's model are so pervasive, so institutionalized, and so ingrained in our way of thinking that it doesn't occur to us that anything's wrong. But Jesus gave us a wake-up call and a commission to carry His model into our families, churches, organizations, and cultures. He is the measuring line that tells whether our current traditions and cultures are built on a godly foundation or the satanic one handed down to us.

Even though male privilege existed long before you and I were born, we are still responsible to decide what we will do when confronted with its existence. For many of the privileged in our world, indifference is the tool of choice. Just as Cain was unmoved by God's confrontation with him about the slaying of his brother, when we find out about injustices, we too can sigh deeply to soothe our consciences and then change the channel. But God has provided a call to action in Jesus.

JESUS CRUSHES THE SERPENT'S HEAD

In Genesis 3, God told us that Jesus would be proactive against the schemes of the enemy. Speaking to the serpent about Jesus, He said, "He will crush your head" (v. 15). These glorious words are God's pronouncement against the serpent, which was carried out by Jesus. But Jesus' example leads us down a very different path than the male privilege in Adam's model.

In Philippians 2, we learn about the privileges that Jesus had and how He stewarded them. Paul wrote that we should "have the same mindset as Christ Jesus: who, being in very nature God, did not consider equality with God something to be used to his own advantage; rather, he made himself nothing by taking the very nature of a servant, being made in human likeness" (vv. 5–7). Jesus had many advantages and many privileges. But He set them aside and, instead, came as a servant.

Paul also laid down rights and privileges that were his, even ones that God gave him as a minister of the gospel. As he wrote to the church in Corinth:

> Don't we have the right to food and drink? Don't we have the right to take a believing wife along with us…?

> ...Don't you know that those who serve in the temple get their food from the temple, and that those who serve at the altar share in what is offered on the altar? In the same way, the Lord has commanded that those who preach the gospel should receive their living from the gospel. *But I have not used any of these rights.*
>
> —1 Corinthians 9:4–5, 13–15, emphasis added

Male privilege fights to preserve earthly superiority of men by lording authority over women, whether overtly or covertly. But this kind of relational breakdown is exactly what Jesus came to address.

For example, at the Last Supper, Jesus dined with His disciples and invited them into a covenant. This covenant was based on Jesus laying down His rights and privileges as the Son of God and serving them. But immediately following the meal, "the disciples bickered over which one of them would be considered the greatest in the kingdom" (Luke 22:24, TPT). Jesus' response was to reiterate His example from the Last Supper:

> Jesus interrupted their argument, saying, "The kings and men of authority in this world rule oppressively over their subjects, claiming that they do it for the good of the people. They are obsessed with how others see them. But this is not your calling. You will lead by a different model. The greatest one among you will live as one called to serve others without honor. The greatest honor and authority is reserved for the one who has a servant heart. The leaders who are served are the most important in your eyes, but

in the kingdom, it is the servants who lead. Am I not here with you as one who serves you?"

—LUKE 22:25–27, TPT

His call is clear: forsake the worldly view of greatness, and follow Him. When we decide to take action against male privilege and the impacts of the fall, there is a temptation to *pick up* Adam's tools and the serpent's methods to do it, but the way of Jesus starts by disarming ourselves and *laying down* our rights. This was how Jesus overcame the fall of humankind—He laid down His rights, was crucified, and went into the grave with the Adamic systems in tow.

Men in privileged places need to resist the initial urge to "fix it" in our own might and power (Zech. 4:6). Instead of seeking to accomplish victory for our sisters through our own efforts, we must go to the cross for ourselves. Instead of merely giving lip service to women's empowerment, Jesus is calling men to lay down their privileges, to surrender their advantages, and to die to an Adamic system that perpetuates their rule over women. Only then can men step into resurrection life alongside their sisters.

FIGHT FOR WOMEN

This resurrection life is not only for a husband and his marriage, but it is also so that he can become an agent of change to impact the lives of men and women around him. The choice to adopt Jesus' model must also spill out of our marriages and into the way that we relate to others, including the way women are treated. This is demonstrated in the life and ministry of John the Baptist, and it's called becoming a friend of the Bridegroom.

The Book of John describes John the Baptist as the Bridegroom's friend, who was involved in the preparations for Jesus and His bride. John refused to draw people to himself but constantly pointed the bride to the Bridegroom. Many historical paintings of John the Baptist show him pointing upwards or outwards, fulfilling his life calling to connect people to Jesus. His role is different than that of a husband, but it helps us understand the heart of the Bridegroom not only for individual marriages but for humanity.

John the Baptist was a lot like a best man. He was closely involved in Jesus' relationship with the bride, but he never confused himself for the groom, nor did he try to direct the bride to himself. John was loyal to Jesus, and from that loyalty came a pure love and appreciation for His bride. When the crowds around John began to turn and follow Jesus instead, John seemed to readily accept it by replying,

> A person can receive only what is given them from heaven.... The bride belongs to the bridegroom. The friend who attends the bridegroom waits and listens for him, and is full of joy when he hears the bridegroom's voice. That joy is mine.
>
> —JOHN 3:27, 29–30

John represents our individual call to connect people with God's salvation, healing, and deliverance. The friend of the Bridegroom lays down his rights and goes to war against anything that hinders Jesus' love relationship with His bride. This includes fighting for our wives and marriages, as well as fighting against the hostility and hatred of women.

One inspiring example of a friend of the Bridegroom is William Booth, cofounder of the Salvation Army. In his final address at Royal

Albert Hall in London, Booth spoke these rousing words as a friend of the Bridegroom:

> While Women weep, as they do now, I'll fight; while children go hungry, as they do now I'll fight; while men go to prison, in and out, in and out, as they do now, I'll fight; while there is a poor lost girl upon the streets, while there remains one dark soul without the light of God, I'll fight, I'll fight to the very end![4]

Jesus' model was first intended for His bride, so husbands adopting it in their marriages must also be committed to Jesus' bride. The choice to follow Jesus in loving our wives must also spill out into care and action in our relationships and areas of influence, the places His bride resides. This is how we become a friend of the Bridegroom in the order of John the Baptist—in our devotion to Jesus, the well-being of His bride becomes a top priority for us. What God forms in us through our marriage at home, He wants to export to the world.

Men walking in Adam's model will not be filled with joy when they hear the Bridegroom's voice because they're clinging to the old system that Jesus overcame. This is the corrupted leadership style that perpetuates male privilege, which sacrifices women to maintain the male-only leadership culture. But the friend of the Bridegroom refuses to rule over or dominate Jesus' bride. May we not be found fighting against Jesus to defend a satanic system of hostility toward women.

I believe that when the heart of the Bridegroom is formed in us, we will not only follow Jesus to restore side-by-side connection and commission with our wives, but we will get a vision for all of God's sons and daughters being able to work together. This collaboration will be built on mutual, self-giving love that champions connection and celebrates each other's success. This will not only be active support and celebration of women, but it will also dismantle systems built under Adam's legacy that keep women under the effects of the fall. Fighting for women does not mean the tearing down of men or the independence of women; it means establishing God's intended relational dynamic for men and women as modeled in the garden and clarified by Jesus. This is men and women who collaborate, cooperate, and partner in shared leadership—and it's worth fighting for.

LEAVE A LEGACY

A progenitor is someone who starts something new, especially in the context of a family. The word breaks down to *pro*, which means forward, and *genitor*, which means to beget or produce. A progenitor is an originator, a forebearer, or a forefather. Progenitors begin something in their families that continues forward or perpetuates after them. They leave a legacy.

From another perspective, if you can credit something in your life to someone who came before you, that person would be considered a progenitor. For some, it may be the first person in the family to obtain a college degree. For others, it may be the alcoholism that has been in your family since your grandparents divorced. We all have an inheritance, both good and bad, from the decisions of those that have gone before us.

Adam was a progenitor, and part of his legacy is a fallen marriage and a broken home. His trajectory from pride all the way to separation did not stop with him. It rolled down over the generations like a waterfall. Adam's legacy is that of a fallen husband, and his personal choices impact all those who came after him.

Joseph was also a progenitor. His legacy was unique from his family line; he did not merely perpetuate the decisions made in previous generations, but rather, he charted a new course. He embraced humility, he submitted himself to God, he identified as Mary's husband, and he served her. Joseph was used by God to show a pattern in which married couples can step into a shared purpose, and the impact of his life can be seen throughout history.

Jesus, the "pioneer and perfecter of faith," was most definitely a progenitor (Heb. 12:2). He lived agape love and sacrificed His life to again have intimate connection with His bride, the church. At the cross, He laid down His rights, privileges, and entitlements as God and died an undeserved death. He crucified the male-only leadership style that resulted from the fall and was resurrected, extending the invitation of union to the church. He invites husbands to follow His example by loving our wives selflessly and pursuing union with them.

We all inherited good or bad things from the choices of those before us. But now we have been handed the baton for our generation, and the question is, what are we going to do with it? We will all leave a legacy formed by the choices that we make. Some of us also have the opportunity to become progenitors by establishing the model of Jesus in our lives and in our families for the first time. Just as God presented Adam with the tree of life and the tree of the knowledge of good and evil, He presents us with a choice.

Future generations will receive an inheritance from you and me. And part of that inheritance will be determined by which model we choose to follow as husbands. Those decisions will start in our individual hearts, and from there, they will ripple out to our marriages, our families, and our world.

What is God calling you to change in your life? What legacy do you want to leave? Whose example will you follow?

> Let us throw off everything that hinders and the sin that so easily entangles. And let us run with perseverance the race marked out for us, fixing our eyes on Jesus, the pioneer and perfecter of faith. For the joy set before him he endured the cross, scorning its shame, and sat down at the right hand of the throne of God. Consider him who endured such opposition from sinners, so that you will not grow weary and lose heart.
>
> —Hebrews 12:1–3

ANSWER THE CALL

We all have choices. And from those choices we reap consequences, for better or for worse. Through my study of Adam, Joseph, and Jesus, I compiled a list of decisions for myself. I'm also extending to you what I believe is an invitation from Jesus presented through the Bible. I'm honored to have shared these truths with you, and I challenge you to answer the 5:25 call. I encourage you to take up the challenge and bring honor to Jesus and transformation to our world through it. I encourage you to read through these declarations and to take ownership of them for yourself. Declaring these over yourself on a daily basis is a powerful way to begin taking ground in your personal life. I also encourage you to sit down with your spouse and create a similar list of "we" statements that you both agree on for your marriage. If you are not married, I encourage you to still go through these declarations and take in the 5:25 call. You can also create a list of identity statements for yourself along the same lines that will help set the direction of your heart and life. Take a moment right now to invite the Holy Spirit to bring transformation to your heart as you choose to answer this 5:25 call. Then join me in making these declarations out loud.

THE 5:25 CALL DECLARATION

> This day, I choose to turn from any fallen views of marriage and of being a husband that have been handed to me. I turn to Jesus to lead me, empower me, and transform me into the man and husband He has called me to be. I love Jesus, I live close to Him, and through Him I can become the man and husband I am called to be. And to this end, I declare:
>
> I forsake the pride of Adam's fallen model, along with all of its satanic roots and fruits. Habitual sin, ungodly generational patterns, and excuses of powerlessness end with me. By the power of the Holy Spirit and the blood of Jesus, I throw off familiar sins along with the temptation to blame God, my wife, or my life circumstances. I take personal responsibility for my life.
>
> - I forsake all pride and ungodly independence from God and my wife.
> - I refuse to partner with insecurity and fear, as well as the behaviors that come from them, such

as hiding myself from others and seeking to control others.
- I refuse to withdraw emotionally or to sabotage my relationships through self-protection, blame, and manipulation.
- I refuse to allow secrecy and secret sin into my life. I reject the lies that my sin won't hurt anyone and that no one will ever know. I seek out others whom I can share my struggles with, and I give them permission to hold me accountable in those areas.
- I refuse to promote ungodly separation from my spouse instead of the intimate connection we were created for.

I embrace the model of humility and service embodied in the life of Joseph, the husband of Mary.

- I embrace true humility that requires vulnerability, honesty, and connection with God and my wife.
- I submit to God's leadership in my life, and I obey His voice. I prioritize faithfulness to Jesus over my reputation.
- I embrace my identity as the husband of my wife and all that it entails. I am united with my wife, and I will not allow anything to bring separation to our shared identity.
- I find ways to serve, support, and champion my wife. I refuse to treat her as inferior. I make

room for my wife to pursue her dreams and passions and to fulfill her God-given callings. I celebrate her successes, especially when they exceed my own.

I pick up my cross and follow Jesus into His original design and intent for me as a man and husband. I choose to love my wife as Christ loved the church by giving up my life for her and pursuing union with her.

- My love for my wife is a stream of devotion, affection, and commitment. My love stays "on" regardless of her actions, words, or reciprocation. I refuse to expose her weakness and mistakes, I honor and protect her. I love her because I love her because I love her.
- I express my love for my wife in a way that can be clearly seen through my thoughts, words, and actions. I refuse to be satisfied by a mere willingness to sacrifice for her; I give up my life for her. My yes to her is an unequivocal no to all others. I do not entertain things that hinder our love relationship. Past identities, privileges, and entitlements that won't come under the umbrella of this union are left in the grave.
- I am a one-woman man, and that woman is my wife. My union with her is my closest human relationship, and I proactively pursue greater connection and intimacy with her. There's room

for both of us to be powerful, and we use our power to serve each other. Resurrection power and Holy Spirit empowerment are my inheritance as I embrace the cross.

I apply the model of Jesus into each area of my life, not only to be a godly husband but to fight for women and to leave a godly legacy.

- I choose to lay down my rights and to follow Jesus. I lay down the benefits and advantages that come from being a man in a male-privileged society, and I shake off the complacency that comes with it.
- I refuse to partner with satanic systems of hatred and hostility toward women, whether blatant or subtle. I choose to fight on behalf of women as a friend of the Bridegroom, and I fight against the things that fight against my sisters and keep them from their God-given destiny.
- I set my heart to be a Christlike example for those around me and to leave a godly legacy for the generations after me.

Jesus is my Lord, and I submit every area of my life to Him. I set my heart to answer the 5:25 call and to be like Him. I depend on Jesus for my life and to become the man and husband He has called me to be.

REFLECTION QUESTIONS

- What are the main characteristics of the 5:25 call?
- Do you identify with any of those characteristics? How so?
- What concepts in this chapter resonated with you the most?
- How do you see male privilege in your life and culture? How does it impact women?
- What legacy do you want to leave?

ACTIVATION

- Speak the 5:25 call declaration out loud, with your heart.
- Complete the prayer guide at the end of this book.

Epilogue

As I share my final thoughts on the 5:25 call and God's design for husbands, I am aware of the fact that I, myself, am a man writing to an audience of men and husbands. It would be easy to develop a sense of satisfaction just because men are being taught and mobilized to represent Jesus in their marriages and spheres of influence. But if we stop there, then we've only developed a male-centered solution that still smacks of Adam's model, and we've stopped short of Jesus' goal. A male-centered solution is incomplete and contains only partial truth. A male-centered solution is no solution at all. Jesus' solution to the fall was centered around union and co-ruling. He wasn't satisfied until His bride was fully alive and by His side, participating, collaborating, and co-reigning with Him.

In the same way, I want to wrap up *The 5:25 Call: God's Design for Husbands* by reminding us all that we cannot break free of Adam's lonely model using Adam's lonely methods. I've intentionally focused this book on the responsibility of men and husbands because it's an aspect of marriage that is many times overlooked or omitted. But the solution to the fall, modeled by Jesus, needs women and is doomed to fail without them. Just as Jesus expects His bride to be built up, mature, and "attaining to the whole measure of the fullness of Christ" (Eph.

4:13), so should men in the body of Christ take a position that insists on women being built up, mature, and reaching the full stature of who they are in God. We need all of His bride to be free, activated, and empowered. This includes the full expression of the women of God and the unique fingerprint of the Creator that they carry.

We need a revelation of the poverty of male-only leadership, as well as contrition of heart over the dynamic that God called "not good" from the beginning. We cannot give only lip service to the need for women to be raised up. We need to perceive and grieve over the limping body of Christ when only part of her has permission to be fully alive. We need to hunger for and heartily pursue the authentic and fully feminine presence, participation, and contribution of our sisters.

My prayer is that as men take up the 5:25 call, the result will be the proactive empowerment of women and genuine partnership with them. I desire that our pursuit of Jesus' call as husbands will lead us to discover our valiant role of fighting for women and co-reigning alongside them. Let's do our part to leave legacies that demonstrate God's design for both husbands and wives, men and women. May our lives and marriages reflect God's design, "a great and sacred mystery—meant to be a vivid example of Christ and his church" (Eph. 5:32, TPT).

May God bless you as you step into His design for husbands found in the 5:25 call.

—Mitch Luse

Prayer Guide

This prayer guide is designed to facilitate an encounter between you and God that will enable you to take hold of the 5:25 call, laying aside hindrances, and experiencing what God has to offer husbands and men in relation to marriage and women.

TIPS ON USING THE PRAYER GUIDE

Location

Choose a location where you can remain uninterrupted for a designated period of time. Inform those around you that you plan to consecrate that time and space to Jesus for this process. Pray over the space, that God would fill it with His presence.

Materials

Get a pen and paper, or a device with a word processor. Plan to write! Writing things down as you go through the prayer guide will help you track what you are hearing. Writing will also give greater definition and longevity to the revelation you are receiving.

Method

You can engage the prayer guide on your own and/or in a group. Choose the method that works best for you. You are welcome to go through the prayer guide more than once using different approaches.

- **Alone with Jesus (one sitting):** Set aside two hours to work through the full prayer guide in one sitting.
- **Alone with Jesus (multiple sittings):** Set aside twenty to twenty-five minutes each day on a Monday-to-Friday to work through the prayer guide in five days, one section at a time.
- **With a group:** Coordinate a group that can work through the prayer guide together. Cover one section of the book and its corresponding prayer component at each gathering.

For the Unmarried

While the prayer guide focuses on husbands, it has application to all men. If you are unmarried, you remain a critical part of God's call to men as it relates to women! You can ask questions in prayer related to women rather than "wives." All men are encouraged to engage this prayer process, adapting it where needed.

PRAYER GUIDE FOUNDATIONS

The following are the foundations used in the prayer guide. Please read through these before engaging the prayer guide. These are included to provide an understanding of the components of prayers outlined in the guide and instructions on how to engage the prayer process.

God's Voice

> Man shall not live on bread alone, but on every word that comes from the mouth of God.
>
> —MATTHEW 4:4

> My sheep hear My voice, and I know them, and they follow Me.
>
> —JOHN 10:27 NASB

God's voice is an important component of the prayer guide. When you ask God a question, pause afterwards and pay attention to what you see, sense, feel or hear from Him. God speaks in a variety of ways. You may have a mental picture, a word that comes to mind, a physical sensation, or receive in a different way. Take notes of what God is speaking to you.

Honor

> "Then neither do I condemn you," Jesus declared. "Go now and leave your life of sin."
>
> —JOHN 8:11

It is "God's kindness that leads to repentance" (Rom. 4:4). If you start feeling condemnation and guilt, surrender these quickly to Jesus and keep moving forward in the prayer process. Jesus' position towards you in this process is honor. He calls you worthy. He is present to receive you, and bring you forward in your own story with a crown of honor for your valiant courage in daring to change.

Forgiveness

> "In anger his master handed him over to the jailers to be tortured, until he should pay back all he owed. This is how my heavenly Father will treat each of you unless you forgive your brother or sister from your heart."
>
> —MATTHEW 18:34-35

The ungodly patterns in your life were likely taught to you by someone else. Judgements and unforgiveness that you hold against those people can unknowingly become a prison of bitterness from which you develop the same patterns. As you identify those who taught you ungodly patterns, forgive those people from the heart. Be specific in your forgiveness prayers. When you are able to view those same people with compassion, that is often a sign that forgiveness has been fully realized.

Beliefs

> Do not conform to the pattern of this world, but be transformed by the renewing of your mind. Then you will be able to test and approve what God's will is—his good, pleasing and perfect will.
>
> —ROMANS 12:2

Your behaviors are often a demonstration of your beliefs. As stated in Proverbs, "For as he thinks within himself, so he is" (23:7 NASB). As you identify ungodly beliefs you have on this topic, you are invited to renounce them and embrace the truth. This work in prayer begins forging new pathways in your brain that will empower new patterns in your life. You will not always be able to self-identify lies you believe, as they may be quite familiar. Ask the Holy Spirit (and others you trust) to help identify your blind spots. For each lie you renounce, ask God for a corresponding truth. Write the truths down. Turn the truths into declarations that you can revisit in the process of renewing your mind.

Exchanges

> The Spirit of the Sovereign Lord is on me... [to] provide for those who grieve in Zion – to bestow on them a crown of beauty instead of ashes, the oil of joy instead of mourning, and a garment of praise instead of a spirit of despair.
>
> —Isaiah 61:1, 3

For many people, areas where the enemy has oppressed them actually prophesy of places that God has intended for glory. The enemy wants to shut down your call and destroy your legacy, but Jesus came with a divine exchange for that scheme. The ungodly patterns you are familiar with were likely demonically constructed, perhaps over generations, to keep you from specific gifts and calls that are on your life.

Jesus is offering to empower your call and use you to leave a glorious legacy. As you surrender things to Jesus in this prayer process, ask Him what He wants to give you in exchange. Focus not on what you are leaving behind, but on what He is calling you into!

THE 5:25 CALL PRAYER GUIDE

Part 1—Adam: The Pride of a Husband

The five attributes of Adam's model are pride, insecurity and fear, self-protection, secrecy, and separation. For each of them, pray through the following steps, inserting the attribute and other information as needed:

Father God, is there any [attribute] in my life as a man/husband?

- Holy Spirit, where did I learn this?
- Jesus, whom do I need to forgive?
    - I choose to forgive [name of person] for [what you need to forgive the person for]. (Matthew 6:12)
    - I choose to cancel the debt they owe me. (Matthew 18)
    - I give up my right to be paid back. (Romans 12:9)
    - Jesus, how do You see this person?
    - Jesus, is there anyone else I need to forgive? [Repeat process if needed.]

Father God, is there a lie that I believe about [attribute]?

- I choose to renounce the lie that [attribute] is [lie].
- Father God, what is the truth?

Jesus, I repent for any way that I have partnered with [attribute].

- I repent on behalf of myself and my family line for any participation with [attribute].
- I choose to break any agreement or communication with a spirit of [attribute].
- I choose to sever any connection with [attribute], and I renounce it now.
- I give [attribute] to You, Jesus.
- What do You want to give me in exchange?

Part 2—Joseph: The Humility of a Husband

The attributes of Joseph's model include humility, submission to God, identifying as a husband, and serving his wife.

Jesus, make me a humble man, fully submitted to You.

- Jesus, will You show me what I have done well as a husband?
- Holy Spirit, what are three ways that I can promote and support my wife's call?
- Father God, You know the dreams and aspirations of my heart, and I choose to surrender them to You today. I surrender to You the expectation that my wife's call and dreams revolve around me. My dreams submitted to Jesus include [list your dreams].
- Jesus, how do You view my wife's call?

Jesus, what are the old identities I gave up when I became a married man?

- I repent for any way I have continued to identify with those things.
- I renounce the lie that I am missing out now that I am married.
- Jesus, what is the truth?
- Father God, how do You view my identity as a married man?

Holy Spirit, I choose to take off any ungodly lenses through which I've viewed my wife and my role of serving her, and I give up my right to insist on my way.

- Holy Spirit, what is important to my wife? What is not important to her?
- How can I serve my wife in a way that she will feel loved?
- How can I serve my wife in a way that You are glorified?

Part 3—Jesus: The Love of a Husband

The primary attributes of Jesus' model include agape love, self-sacrifice, and union with His bride.

Jesus, has there been anyone in my life who was supposed to love me but did not or who was not safe for me?

- I choose to forgive [name of person] for not teaching me about godly love.
- Jesus, I hand to You any broken experiences with love from my past.
- What do You want to give me in exchange for my marriage?

Father God, what is Your love for me like?

- Father God, what is Your love for my wife like?
- Father God, what is Your love for us as a married couple like?

Holy Spirit, what is selfishness in marriage protecting me from?

- Father God, will I be safe if I surrender self-protection to You?
- Jesus, I choose to hand over any self-protection or selfishness in my marriage.
- What do You give me to meet my needs without selfishness?

Father God, what is Your dream for my marriage?

- What spheres have You called us to influence together?
- How can I empower my wife and give her authority?
- What does it look like for both of us to be powerful?

Part 4—The Call

The 5:25 call is ultimately about loving your wife "just as Christ loved the church and gave himself up for her" (Eph. 5:25).

Jesus, what is Your heart for women?

- What is my role in fulfilling the desires of Your heart for women?
- I repent for any apathy I have felt or shown in regards to Your heart for women, and I give my apathy to You, Jesus.
- What do You want to give me in exchange?

Express to Jesus the patterns you have seen in your family line and culture related to men and husbands.

- Express to Jesus how you want to be a progenitor of new patterns. Write your thoughts in a notebook or journal.
- What legacy do you want to leave as a husband to your family and the generations after you? Write your thoughts in a notebook or journal.
- Read the 5:25 call out loud from the end of chapter 5 as a declaration.

Part 5—The 5:25 Call Twelve-Week Challenge

The twelve-week challenge is an opportunity for you to keep the shared vision you and your wife have for your marriage at the forefront of your thoughts as you seek to love your wife as Christ loved the church.

With your wife, write out a shared vision statement for your marriage in a notebook or journal. Pray over it together.

- Save the 5:25 call declaration and your marriage vision statement together in a place where you can access them easily.
- Read the 5:25 call declaration and your marriage vision statement out loud at least once a week for three months.
- Every time you read them out loud, make a note of the date in your notebook or journal, along with anything else that you sense from God.
- When you successfully complete the challenge, share your testimony and experience with me through my website at mitchluse.com and through social media with a picture and #525Call.

The prayer guide foundations and corresponding principles are derived from ConnectUp, a ministry founded by Mitch and Katie Luse. For more information about ConnectUp Prayer, including resources, opportunities to receive personal prayer ministry, and training information, visit www.iconnectup.net.